STUDIES IN ECONOMIC AND SOCIAL HISTORY

This series, specially commissioned by the Economic History Society, provides a guide to the current interpretations of the key themes of economic and social history in which advances have recently been made or in which there has been significant debate.

Originally entitled 'Studies in Economic History', in 1974 the series had its scope extended to include topics in social history, and the new series title, 'Studies in Economic and Social History', signalises this development.

The series gives readers access to the best work done, helps them to draw their own conclusions in major fields of study, and by means of the critical bibliography in each book guides them in the selection of further reading. The aim is to provide a springboard to further work rather than a set of pre-packaged conclusions or short-cuts.

ECONOMIC HISTORY SOCIETY

The Economic History Society, which numbers around 3000 members, publishes the *Economic History Review* four times a year (free to members) and holds an annual conference. Enquiries about membership should be addressed to the Assistant Secretary, Economic History Society, P.O. Box 190, 1 Greville Road, Cambridge, CB1 3QG. Full-time students may join at special rates.

D0322082

STUDIES IN ECONOMIC AND SOCIAL HISTORY
Edited for the Economic History Society by L. A. Clarkson

PUBLISHED

OTHER TITLES IN PREPARATION

Housing in Urban Britain 1780–1914: Class, Capitalism and Construction

Prepared for
The Economic History Society by

RICHARD RODGER
Senior Lecturer in Economic and Social History
University of Leicester

MACMILLAN

First published 1989

Published by
MACMILLAN EDUCATION LTD
Houndmills, Basingstoke, Hampshire RG21 2XS
and London
Companies and representatives
throughout the world

British Library Cataloguing in Publication Data
Rodger, Richard, 1947–
Housing in Urban Britain 1780–1914 : class,
capitalism and construction.—(Studies in
economic and social history).
1. Great Britain. Urban regions. Housing,
1780–1914
I. Title II. Economic History Society
III. Series
363.5'0941
ISBN 0–333–38708–2

Filmsetting by Vantage Photosetting Co. Ltd,
Eastleigh and London
Printed in Hong Kong

Series Standing Order

If you would like to receive future titles in this series as they are published, you can make use of our standing order facility. To place a standing order please contact your bookseller or, in case of difficulty, write to us at the address below with your name and address and the name of the series. Please state with which title you wish to begin your standing order. (If you live outside the United Kingdom we may not have the rights for your area, in which case we will forward your order to the publisher concerned.)

Customer Services Department, Macmillan Distribution Ltd
Houndmills, Basingstoke, Hampshire, RG21 2XS, England.

Contents

Acknowledgements

I should like to thank Martin Daunton, Peter Fearon, Paul Laxton, Lynn Lees and Tom Weiss for their valued criticisms of an earlier draft. To Ted Wilson and the Joyce and Elizabeth Hall Center for the Humanities, University of Kansas, I am particularly grateful for the encouragement and financial support to enable me to complete the typescript. I am grateful to Academic Press for permission to reproduce Figures 1 and 2 and to Leicester University Press for Figure 4. This book, begun in an attic and completed in a cellar dwelling, is dedicated to my parents, whose breadth of housing experience never lost sight of the importance of the home.

Note on References

References in the text within square brackets relate to the items in the Bibliography, and are followed by page numbers in italics. Other references in the text, numbered consecutively throughout the book, relate to sources not given in the bibliography, and are itemised in the notes and references section.

Editor's Preface

When this series was established in 1968 the first editor, the late Professor M. W. Flinn, laid down three guiding principles. The books should be concerned with important fields of economic history; they should be surveys of the current state of scholarship rather than a vehicle for the specialist views of the authors, and above all, they were to be introductions to their subject and not 'a set of pre-packaged conclusions'. These aims were admirably fulfilled by Professor Flinn and by his successor, Professor T. C. Smout, who took over the series in 1977. As it passes to its third editor and approaches its third decade, the principles remain the same.

Nevertheless, times change, even though principles do not. The series was launched when the study of economic history was burgeoning and new findings and fresh interpretations were threatening to overwhelm students – and sometimes their teachers. The series has expanded its scope, particularly in the area of social history – although the distinction between 'economic' and 'social' is sometimes hard to recognise and even more difficult to sustain. It has also extended geographically; its roots remain firmly British, but an increasing number of titles is concerned with the economic and social history of the wider world. However, some of the early titles can no longer claim to be introductions to the current state of scholarship; and the discipline as a whole lacks the heady growth of the 1960s and early 1970s. To overcome the first problem a number of new editions, or entirely new works, have been commissioned – some have already appeared. To deal with the second, the aim remains to publish up-to-date introductions to important areas of debate. If the series can demonstrate to students and their teachers the importance of the discipline of economic and social history and excite its further study, it will continue the task so ably begun by its first two editors.

The Queen's University of Belfast   L. A. CLARKSON
                                          General Editor

1   Introduction: an Urban Framework

By the 1840s the widespread existence of defective housing in cities throughout Britain was known and the term 'slum' had assumed common usage [Dyos, 1967, *8*]. The Health of Towns Report (1840) referred to the 'miserable and neglected state of the dwellings of the poor' and, with particular reference to working-class housing in Liverpool and Manchester, remarked that it was 'scarcely possible to conceive any construction more prejudicial to the health of the inhabitants'. *The Times* carried similarly vivid accounts. But both newspapers and official enquiries, while cataloguing housing defects – principally structural weaknesses, poor drainage and sewage – were also aware of the underlying political economy of housing. The Health of Towns Commissioners noted explicitly that, despite their contribution to economic growth the working class, 'by whose hands these riches were created' were 'condemned through no fault of their own' to housing conditions where it was 'impracticable for them to preserve health or decency . . . or keep themselves or their children from moral and physical contamination'.[1]

The problem of working-class housing in mid-Victorian British cities therefore was not simply a matter of building more and better dwellings for artisans; it was rooted in the structure of the new industrial society itself. The unprecedented, sustained and at times explosive expansion of city populations in the first four decades of the nineteenth century rendered wholly inadequate the existing arrangements for urban living. The cumulative pressure of numbers prompted a material breakdown of urban society as reflected in the state of public health and in the contamination of food and water supplies [Wohl, 1983, *6*].

Against a setting of dramatic industrial and urban change, events such as cholera outbreaks and radical protest movements

1

had, by the beginning of Victoria's reign, sufficiently alarmed middle-class interests to instigate enquiries into the nature of urban society. Books, pamphlets and parliamentary commissions in the 1830s and 1840s revealed a social transformation within British cities in the wake of industrialisation, and in particular addressed a trio of related issues: sanitation, housing and employment conditions [Gauldie, 1974, *101*]. Particularly alarming was the morbidity of the population which by the 1840s was systematically linked to housing conditions. Case-studies and quantification were preludes to the formulation of social policy, yet that policy was itself based upon a *laissez-faire* economic doctrine where legislative intervention was confined mainly to the physical and moral conditions of women and children in the workplace in an attempt to minimise the destructive effect of the factory system on twin Victorian ideals – family and home.

Accounts of housing in the first half of the nineteenth century concentrated on the spatial distribution of death and disease [Dennis, 1984, *48*]. Contemporaries identified significant variations in adult male life expectancy between town and country and between social classes within cities. What emerged unequivocally was a correlation between morality and disease on the one hand, and housing and sanitary conditions on the other. Innumerable stark accounts of housing conditions, presented in statistical tables, maps and oral evidence, provided conclusive proof of a geographical division within British cities so that by the 1840s they had become socially and residentially segregated between rich and poor areas, cleansed and uncleansed streets, and in the minds of some, between an indigenous population and the Irish.

Contemporary explanations of defective housing conditions varied enormously. Intemperance, idleness and injudicious expenditure were commonly advanced to explain poor housing. More liberal interpretations acknowledged such behaviour as understandable, though unacceptable, forms of escapism from oppressive housing. Others, such as Chadwick in his *Report on the Sanitary Condition of the Labouring Population of Great Britain* (1842), incorporated economic factors in their explanations: deficient housing and sanitation fostered disease, disease produced poverty, both through interrupted income arising from ill-

2

health and by increasing the numbers of widows and orphans dependent on poor relief, and ultimately intensified the burden on ratepayers. Whether the pig created the sty or the sty created the pig, a contemporary paraphrasing of the causes of poor housing captured the political dimensions of the problems which also underlay Engels' *The Condition of the Working Classes in England* (1845), Faucher's *Manchester in 1844*, Disraeli's *Sybil* (1845) and other accounts centred on rich/poor, bourgeois/ proletarian, employer/employee divisions. This ideological perspective on residential segregation has variously been interpreted as an abandonment by the middle and upper classes of a traditional responsibility for workers' welfare, as a dereliction of duty in setting social norms and imposing control mechanisms on the working class, and as a liberalising of the working class from repressive traditions and behaviour. Whatever the differences of interpretation, Victorians further employed the observable correlation between morbidity and housing conditions to explain also atheism, radicalism and immorality [Harvey, 1973, *131–43*; Dennis, 1984, *49*; Engels, 1887, *23, 43, 74–7*].

Largely as a response to the degenerate city, and assisted by rising prosperity and the emergence of urban public transport – successively horse buses, trams, local railways and in London the Underground – the middle class began to withdraw from congested town centre living from the 1820s. Propelled by an aversion to contamination, moral and physical, the middle classes increasingly quit downtown residence and approached suburban life with an air of optimism and relief, reinforced by their deliberate efforts to separate home and work. Many properties vacated by the middle class were occupied by artisans and the petit bourgeoisie while others were subdivided for multiple working-class dwellings. As a result, a clearly defined segregation of residential areas, based on income differentials, geographically polarised urban society by the middle of the nineteenth century [Dennis, 1984, *73*]. Earlier formulations of this process have identified the town as a series of concentric circles, with slum, factory and warehouse at the core, 'respectable' working-class housing in the next ring, and middle-class villas at the perimeter [Alonso, 1960, *156*; Whitehand, 1987, *30*]. Though rather inflexible and with a disregard for local topography, the idea of distinct zones captured the essence of the disintegration of towns into slums and suburbs. Crucially, this centrifugal suburbanising trend distanced those comfortably off from direct, daily confrontation with squalid housing, poverty and moral degeneracy, and reinforced their disinclination as the urban political elite to address fundamental issues central to improvements in working-class living conditions. It became easier to overlook the squalor of central slums from the comfortable distance of a suburban villa than when occupying an older town house in the core of the city.

Despite the minimal interventionist stance of the urban elite as reflected in weak, permissive housing statutes and under-pinned by ratepayers' pressure for economies in local authority expenditure, the character of housing altered appreciably during the nineteenth century. Pronounced separation of low- and high-status housing areas, regulated parallel lines of terraced housing, standardised monotony of design, colour and visual impact, privatised space immediately surrounding properties, and the redefinition of domestic routines following the introduction of piped water and gas, fundamentally chang-ed the nature of housing in the century preceding the First World War. For many the house became less a shelter and more a home. Such physical changes were both a reaction and a stimulus to broader social changes – for example the emergence of the nuclear family and the Victorian idealisation of family life. But there were, too, conscious efforts to improve the quality of housing in the second half of the nineteenth century. Philanthropic and charitable institutions, employers' housing and working men's building cooperatives illustrated individual and collective pragmatism in addressing housing needs. Build-ing bye-laws and slum clearance programmes were indicative of a reluctant posture amongst municipal authorities in connec-tion with qualitative improvements in housing, though from the 1880s this attitude gave way, if not to an ideological shift, to a more enthusiastic embrace of council housebuilding, utopian planning and garden city ideals. That so many initiatives were necessary in the mid- and late-Victorian years demonstrates both the immensity and persistence of housing inadequacies, and differences in the Victorians' interpretations of the problem. A concerted attack was never forthcoming. Only in the aftermath of the First World War was there a political will to identify the scale of minimum housing needs and dovetail a building programme to achieve it [Swenarton, 1981, *47*].

2   Urban Expansion and the Pattern of Demand

The reasons for the obstinate nature of the 'housing problem' during the nineteenth century were cast in the circumstances of early urbanisation. Two principal demand factors can be identified: (i) population expansion, and (ii) low wages and weak effective demand for housing.

(i) POPULATION, MIGRATION AND THE CITIES

Though definitional arguments and difficulties of enumeration obscure the exact proportions of the population living in towns of 2500 or more people, an unquestionable transformation of the urban system occurred during the nineteenth century underlining a process already under way [Law, 1967, *130*]. In the early eighteenth century the pattern of towns was essentially that of the Middle Ages: 500–600 small market towns of approximately 500 to 1800 people, with a number of larger and more prominent county towns with legal, ecclesiastical and administrative functions. Five provincial capitals – Norwich, Exeter, Bristol, York and Newcastle – superseded these county towns and, sufficiently remote from metropolitan London, they dominated a complex regional system of communications, cultural and economic activity. This ancient urban hierarchy had been overturned by 1801, and though London continued pre-eminent, and Bristol and Norwich remained in the top ten towns by size, the provincial cities, ports and specialised manufacturing centres supplanted county and small towns [Chalklin, 1976, *25*; Corfield, 1982, *11*].

The urban proportion of the population advanced from approximately 33 per cent in 1801 to 50 per cent in 1851, to 72 per cent in 1891, and to 79 per cent by 1911 (Table 1). This relentless trend nonetheless obscured the spectacular experience

Table 1 Growth Indices for Population, England and Wales 1801–1911

	Total population	Urban population	%Decennial change Total	Urban	Urban % of population
1801	100	100			33.8
1811	114	124	14.0	23.7	36.6
1821	135	160	18.1	29.1	40.0
1831	156	204	15.8	28.0	44.3
1841	179	256	14.3	25.0	48.3
1851	202	322	12.6	25.9	54.0
1861	226	392	11.9	21.6	58.7
1871	255	492	13.2	25.6	65.2
1881	292	604	14.7	22.8	70.0
1891	326	718	11.6	18.8	74.5
1901	366	843	12.2	17.5	78.0
1911	406	946	10.9	12.2	78.9

Source: [Law, 1967, *130*]

of individual towns. Two-thirds of the twelve largest cities in 1871 had experienced their most rapid acceleration in the 1820s; Bristol grew by 70%, Bradford 66%, Salford 56%, Leeds 47%, Liverpool 46%, Manchester 46%, Birmingham 42%, and Sheffield by 41%. Twenty-six Lancashire towns added about a third to their population in each decade between 1820 and 1850, and if this pace was beyond most towns, a 20–30 per cent increase in each census 1801–51, or a tripling of a town's residents over the period was by no means uncommon. Nor was it confined to major urban areas – such diverse places as Runcorn, Huddersfield, Swansea, Burslem and Bilston (Wolverhampton) underwent similar proportionate increases, and Birkenhead, a small town of 1025 people in 1821, tripled in each census 1831, 1841 and 1851. Individual parishes were transformed into seething human concentrations, as in Blackfriars, Glasgow, with a 40 per cent population increase in the 1830s, and many London parishes when in the 1840s one third of a million immigrants descended on the capital [Gauldie, 1974, *83*]. The seven parishes in West Derby (Liverpool) expanded from 12,000 to 153,000 between 1801 and 1851, with Toxteth, Everton and West Derby principally responsible for a decennial percentage increase never below 60 per cent before

7

1851. Concentrated Irish communities existed in many British towns prior to the potato blight; by 1841 the Irish constituted 17 per cent of the Liverpool population, 12 per cent in Manchester and 5–8 per cent in Bradford, Wigan and other northern textile towns where their presence lent a distinctive flavour to specific neighbourhoods [Dennis, 1984, 37].

The exact division of responsibility between natural increase and immigration for this unprecedented urban population expansion before 1850 remains unclear. By 1800 towns were by no means exclusively dependent upon recruitment from the shires, thereby reversing the earlier eighteenth-century pattern where urban population growth relied upon immigrants [Corfield, 1982, 106]. At the introduction of civil registration in the 1840s, which revealed urban birth rates universally above death rates, the continuing flood of immigration was swollen by an element of natural increase in the towns themselves. After 1840, 60 per cent of urban population growth was due to natural increase, and 40 per cent to immigration.[2]

The combined contribution of natural increase and immigration remains the central point of departure for nineteenth-century housing. For 105 ports, manufacturing, mining and metal-working towns whose populations increased approximately 200 per cent between 1801 and 1851, the pressure on housing was of a different magnitude to those 99 county and administrative towns, which though not exempt from such pressure, expanded at almost half that rate (122 per cent). The unquestionable fact is that the urban population increase in the three decades before 1831 was itself more than the total population in 1801. It needed shelter. Unless the construction of new housing was particularly responsive, the health of the migrants exceptional, and urban expansion meticulously controlled, it is not difficult to appreciate why overcrowding developed. The excess of families over houses more than doubled between 1801 and 1871, and if, paradoxically, the number of persons per house was static at 5.6 between 1801 and 1831 and fell sightly to 5.4 in 1841, this can be explained by the subdivision of existing properties, more intensive site development, and by initial suburban moves in the 1820s [Treble (Chapman), 1971, 211; Chalklin, 1974, App. VI]. Acute middle-class perceptions had at an early stage generated genteel inner suburbs – Everton (Liverpool), Edgbaston (Birmingham), Blythswood (Glasgow), Hampstead (London) [Simpson and Lloyd, 1977, *47, 93, 177*; Burnett, 1978, *106*] though it was not long before they too were encroached upon or encircled by continuing urban expansion and residents again moved to remote suburbs with exclusivity protected by constructional standards and transport costs.

Though urban population expansion continued in the second half of the nineteenth century, it posed a lesser problem. This was because, firstly, the decennial increase slackened somewhat (Table 1); secondly, with virtual saturation of central building sites population additions were increasingly housed on peripheral sites, a process assisted by transport developments for the suburbanising middle class; thirdly, this physical expansion engulfed villages and small towns, and thus boundary alterations – a rarity before 1850 – partially accounted for urban population increases; and finally, after 1850 municipalities were not content, as formerly, to allow the environmental implications of continuing population pressure to go unchecked.

(ii) WAGES, EMPLOYMENT AND THE STRUCTURE OF DEMAND

Were increased productivity and economic growth associated with industrialisation transmitted to the working class, and with what effect on housing? Apart from assessments of working conditions and the psychological and physical effects of factory production, shreds of wage-price data suggest only the most marginal improvement in workers' income and consumption patterns between 1750 and 1820. In 1801–3 a pattern of inequality in which 60 per cent of the population earned approximately 20 per cent of national income narrowed only marginally in the course of the nineteenth century.[3] More significantly as far as housing was concerned, there were 'relatively few indications of significant change in levels of real wages . . . before 1810/14.'[4] Recently it has become apparent that once a more disaggregated view of the workforce is taken then 'many workers may have been losers, at least until the 1820s'[5] and even optimistic calculations of real wages[6] date most

9

of the gains to the years 1827–50. This corresponds, for example, with trends in consumption and life expectancy[7] and data on Leeds rentals which increased by 33 per cent 1790–1830 [Rimmer, 1963, *186*]. Even the more generous real wage rather than earnings data thus suggest that for the half century of most rapid urbanisation the workforce had no more to spend on rent, and received less space for it.

Conversely, between 1850 and 1914 cumulative improvements in real wages, whatever the regional variations and methods of calculation, were more than any other factor decisive in advancing the housing condition of the majority of Victorians. During these years the overall real wage increase was approximately 75–80 per cent.[8] A modest decennial real wage advance of about 4 per cent was recorded in the 1850s, accelerating to 12 per cent in the 1860s, 16 per cent in the 1870s, 19 per cent in the 1880s, thereafter the pace slackened, to about 8 per cent in the 1890s, and in 1900–14, years of slight reversal, real wages declined by about 3 per cent. Just as the accumulated contribution of real wages cannot be underestimated in relation to late-Victorian housing improvements, so the virtual absence of real wage advances 1750–1820 was equally decisive. Weak demand for housing ensured mean accommodation.

Rents as a percentage of household expenditure were inversely related to income; the smaller the income, the higher the proportion devoted to rent. Whereas the national average for much of the nineteenth century was about 16 per cent of income spent on rent, for the middle class the figure was 8–10 per cent, for the working class 16–25 per cent, and for the very poor it was about 30 per cent [Gauldie, 1974, *164*; Englander, 1983, *6*]. Although this element of the household budget may have increased after 1880, before that date 85 per cent of the London working class paid a quarter, and 50 per cent between a quarter and a half of their incomes to landlords as rents [Wohl, 1977, *40*]. Moreover, in contrast to the twentieth century, the rented sector accounted for the overwhelming majority of housing accommodation with a modest 14–23 per cent of properties owner-occupied (Swenarton and Taylor, 1985, *375*].

Trends in wages apart, low absolute levels of pay and interrupted income flows determined housing expenditure patterns of a basic nature. In 1900, after half a century of improvement, primary poverty – insufficient wages for subsistence – affected 6.4 per cent of the population of Northampton, 9.9 per cent in York, 11.5 and 15.3 per cent in Warrington and Reading respectively, and 20 per cent in Black Country towns (Treble, 1979, *20*]. Superimposed on the dual problems of low pay and disproportionate rentals was that of interrupted wages for, in the saturated market for unskilled labour, few Victorian workers could expect a lifetime of regular employment. Cyclical depression and technological unemployment confronted all workers, albeit unequally, but for significant elements of the unskilled, casual and seasonal employment had a pervasive impact on consumption patterns, most notably on housing, even though this could be partially offset by earnings from family members, taking in lodgers, and landlords' agreement to rent arrears.

The informal or casual nature of hiring in the nineteenth century is crucial to a comprehension of the behavioural and expenditure patterns of the urban working class. For men, portering, messengering, carting, street selling and general labouring were major areas of irregular employment, engagement for which was customarily by the day, or even half-day [Jones, 1971, *64, 376*]. More specifically, the docks, building trades, gas industry, shoe and clothing trades, coal distribution and confectionery offered periods of intense seasonal activity followed by extended bouts of under- or unemployment. The rag trade particularly, but also box, broom, shoe and comb-making, were for women workers subject to seasonal interruptions. Depending on local variations in the composition of employment, but as a broad indication of the generality of irregular wages, approximately 25 per cent of male workers in late-Victorian Britain could expect interrupted income in the course of a year, levels which were probably greater in the early nineteenth century, though Mayhew's estimates for the 1840s and 1850s of two-thirds of Londoners either irregularly employed or unemployed was probably an overstatement [Jones, 1971, *53*].

The endemic nature of Victorian poverty was captured by Booth's conclusion that, in the 1890s, 30.7 per cent of London's population (Rowntree estimated 27.8 per cent for York) lived in poverty. In a labour-intensive age where fluctuations in business were met by hiring and firing unskilled workers, that is, forcing output adjustments on labour rather than capital, it is not surprising that accommodation reflected the severe pressure on income. In fact two structural features of the labour market were of crucial importance to the quality of workers' housing. Firstly, the employment 'bargain', struck on a daily or half-daily engagement basis, demanded housing in proximity to places of potential work. This requirement was intensified by the timing and rhythm of work itself. Breakfast and lunch breaks could conveniently and economically be taken at home if this was located nearby. But proximity also meant competition with industrial, retailing and commercial land uses, and in view of constraints on working-class wages the amount of space affordable was predictably limited. For these reasons, as previously noted, rents formed a disproportionately high percentage of labourers' incomes. Secondly, to avoid eviction in periods of interrupted employment, the family housing strategy was to rent such space as was consistent with reduced wages in the worst employment periods; accommodation was adjusted to the lowest common denominator of wages, not the average, over the course of the tenancy period [Rodger, 1986, *171*].

By differentiating the components of housing demand on the basis of income flow, apparently contradictory interpretations of the nineteenth-century housing experience may be rationalised. Optimists (Tarn, Burnett, Gauldie, Daunton) point to the introduction of amenities such as running water, gas, WCs, improved structural standards and suburban developments as indications of enhanced housing provision in the Victorian age, especially from the 1860s. The pessimists (Wohl, Stedman Jones, Rodger) do not deny such advances, but argue that, the middle class apart, improvements were confined to the clerks, petit bourgeoisie, artisans and more regularly employed working class. Booth noted that it was not simply the level of wages, but the *predictability* of income and consequently the affordability of a given rent which meant that railway workers were less overcrowded than those paid equivalent wages [Jones, 1971, *53*]. The controversy between optimists and pessimists is therefore less over whether high- or poor-quality housing existed, but more over the changing balance during the course of the century.

12

3 Supply Influences

(i) LANDOWNERSHIP, ESTATE DEVELOPMENT AND HOUSING

Amongst the most prominent urban landowning families were the Bute (Cardiff), Donegall (Belfast), Fitzwilliam and Norfolk (Sheffield), Ramsden (Huddersfield), Derby (Liverpool, Bootle and Bury) and the Sefton and Salisbury families (also Liverpool). Dominating the landownership structure in holiday resorts were the Devonshire (Eastbourne), Radnor (Folkestone), Tapps-Gervis-Meryrick (Bournemouth), Palk, later Haldon (Torquay), Hesketh and Scarisbrick (Southport), Mostyn (Rhyl) and Scarborough (Skegness) families. No less important were institutional landowners – the churches, trusts and colleges such as Dulwich (Camberwell), Eton (Chalcots), Sidney Sussex (Cleethorpes) and St. John's (Oxford) [Cannadine, 1980, *41, 64*].

Were landowners primary influences on housing or mere ciphers of market forces? The sequence of housebuilding involved landowners, developers (laying out streets and drains), builders, and finally landlords, or occupiers, though not uncommonly stages were combined as when landowners were active as developers [Chalklin, 1974, *57*]. While more than twenty forms of tenure existed, estate development in England centred on two principal strategies and tenures, either retaining (leasehold) or relinquishing (freehold) title to land [Dyos, 1961, *87*]. This choice revolved on two further considerations – a landowner's immediate cash needs and his wish to influence future building development. Under the freehold option the landowner sold land outright to developers or builders as one lot or subdivided, thereby ceding all future interest in the property for a lump sum payment. Fragmented and dispersed estates persuaded some landowners of their negligible ability to influence subsequent development and they sold out. Interest in and control over housing quality was accordingly minor.

Alternatively, the option preferred by many landowners was to lease, that is, to retain the title to land and augment its annual value by encouraging building. The landowner leased to a developer or building association on conditions which often specified housing standards and values; the developer could act as builder or subcontract building work, and agreed to pay to the landowner either a fixed rent on each house or an overall rent for the ground leased. An overall rent was preferable since the landowner had only one rental to collect and the developer/builder could reassign rents on each plot at an 'improved' or inflated figure and thus raise capital on security of expected future ground rents. As with freehold the landowner might specify the type and quality of housing constructed, but had greater reason to enforce such stipulations for they influenced subsequent development prospects on his neighbouring sites. Leasing land for building development produced an annual income, a capital gain because retention of the title meant land and the property on it reverted, on expiry of the lease, to the landowner, and it offered rack-renting possibilities, that is, receipt of tenants' house rents worth 5 – 10 times the ground rent charged to the lessee. For example, the Denmark Park estate (London) in 1879 produced annual ground rents of £640, but on expiry produced £4000 p.a. from tenants' house rents [Dyos, 1961, *88*]. In the early nineteenth century the length of lease was considerably shorter than in the later Victorian period – 30 years compared to about 80 years – and so the greater rack-renting frequency diminished landlords' interest in maintenance and adversely affected housing quality.

Charges that leaseholding produced dilapidated housing were not based on reversionary and rack-renting characteristics. Leaseholding also attracted criticism because small speculative builders could, through the improved ground rent device, raise substantial sums for working capital on the basis of a modest outlay on land and while this increased the supply of low-income housing, quality was rarely a major consideration. Freehold tenure also contributed to the housing problem. Again small speculative builders were instrumental, for in buying freehold land outright or even on an instalment basis they were as financially pressed as their counterparts on leasehold estates and intensive site development such as for West Riding back-to-backs and Tyneside flats resulted [Mortimore, 1960, *115*; Daunton, 1983, *66*].

Were tenure and urban landownership fundamental influences on housing design and spatial development in nineteenth-century cities? In 1914, about 60 per cent of urban tenures in the United Kingdom were freehold and the remainder were various types of leasehold [Offer, 1981 , *118*]. Though a blend of tenures existed in most boroughs, some geographical concentrations existed. For example, Leeds, Bradford and West Riding towns were dominated by freehold and Lancashire by long leases. Nevertheless, serious housing deficiencies were not confined to one type of tenure or location. Poorly drained areas were developed for industrial purposes or working-class housing irrespective of who owned the land, how concentrated the ownership was, or the nature of the tenure. By the same token freehold-dominated Leeds and overwhelmingly leasehold Birmingham, produced almost identical middle-class suburbs, Headingley in the former city and Edgbaston in the latter [Cannadine, 1980, *403*]. In Hampstead fractured landownership did not impede homogeneous housing development [Thompson (Simpson and Lloyd), 1977, *110*]. Short-lease development was used for high-status housing by the Bedford estate (London) and for low-income housing by the Norfolk estate in Sheffield [Olsen, 1973, *365*]. Dominant landowners with leasehold controls and reversionary interests, such as with the Bute family in Cardiff, and a fragmented ownership structure, as in Bristol, both produced similar through-terraced housing [Daunton, 1977, *76*; 1983, *78*]. Nor was 'feuing' – the peculiarly Scottish combination of freehold and leasehold tenure systems – associated exclusively with middle- or working-class tenement residence [Rodger, 1983, *200*]. Geographical variations in rent levels bore no simple relation to the concentration of landownership, and overcrowding was not particularly associated in England with one type of tenure.

Systems of tenure, therefore, were simply different methods of achieving a common purpose amongst landowners, the maximisation of yield on an asset – land. Some chose immediate lump sum realisation by means of freehold sale; others preferred an annual income in the form of leasehold ground rents, and if these were higher on working-class properties this reflected the

15

fact that on low-income housing collection was more difficult and reversionary value lower [Thompson, 1974, *366*]. While the precise form of a particular estate, its boundaries, street widths and layout were undoubtedly shaped by landowners who continued by means of parks, exclusive suburbs and holiday resort developments to defend the social tone of an area [Perkin, 1975, *185*], the 'great estates were ultimately constrained by forces of the market' [Cannadine, 1980, *393*; Daunton, 1977, *73*; Thompson (Simpson and Lloyd), 1977, *110*; Olsen, 1976, *13*].

(ii) THE BUILDING INDUSTRY

Nineteenth-century housing has occupied a central position in arguments concerning international capitalist development, formulated on the basis of an economic model of systematic, inverse flows of capital and labour, principally between Britain and North America – the 'Atlantic Economy' hypothesis [Cooney, 1949, *353*; Cairncross, 1953, *209*; Thomas, 1954, *175*]. The alternating mechanism (Table 2), with approximately twenty years between building cycle peaks, supposed that buoyancy in the US economy meant a simultaneous heavy outflow of both investment and emigrants from the UK. Emigration to and investment in the New World impeded domestic investment, both industrial and residential, and the valve controlling this flow of resources was released by the relative attractiveness of transatlantic wages, dividends, profits and interest rates. Higher returns on the European side of the

Table 2   Housebuilding Fluctuations in Britain and America 1870–1913

	UK		US	
Peak	Trough	Peak	Trough	
	1871	1871		
1877			1878	
	1892	1892		
1899			1900	
	1912	1912		

Source: [Thomas; 1954, *103*]

16

Atlantic meant that factors of production remained in the UK. Though advanced in the broader context of Victorian capitalism and international fluctuations for the period 1830–1914, subsequent formulations of the thesis considered it appropriate only from 1870 with the emergence and growing independence of the American economy after the Civil War [Habakkuk, 1962, 25]. Neither chronological span explained the initial housing problem in Britain during the first half of the nineteenth century, and subsequent detailed studies of South Wales, Teesside, London boroughs, the Manchester conurbation, and Scottish towns revealed considerable local housebuilding diversity after 1870 (Figure 1, overleaf) and a consequential lack of synchronisation with international fluctuations [Saul, 1962; Kenwood, 1963; Lewis, 1965]. Local influences on building supplanted the primacy of international fluctuations and a single national building cycle with many cycles systematically linked to local economic prosperity. Thus demand conditions and the internal structure of the building industry were accorded overriding explanatory importance.

(a) Investment in housing

Housebuilding accounted for about one-fifth (21 per cent) of capital formation between 1760 and 1800 (Table 3, overleaf) [Feinstein, 1978, 40] even though late-eighteenth-century industrialisation presented a rash of industrial investment opportunities. For the next thirty years the relative share of housbuilding increased to about one-third above late-eighteenth-century proportions. Wartime interest rates and investors' search for security discouraged industrial investment, but three distributional considerations modified this apparently healthy improvement in residential investment. Firstly, it applied exclusively to new, not to existing, housing. The majority of properties were unaffected by new investment unless it was used to subdivide existing larger properties, thereby converting them into more congested dwellings. Secondly, the residential investment applied across the income strata; it included extensive classical Georgian crescents, squares and villas of the middle class. Thirdly, just as population growth had outstripped residential construction during 1760–1800, it did so again during 1800–40 when population

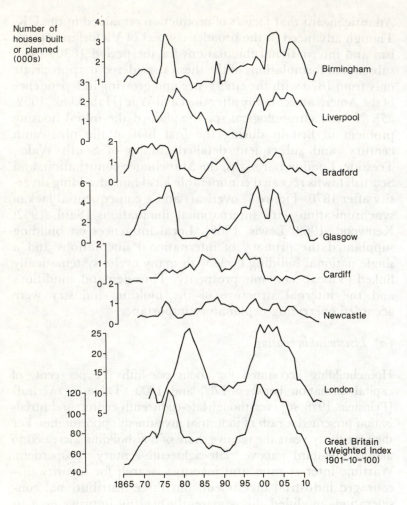

Figure 1   Fluctuations in housebuilding 1865–1913

increased by 156 per cent in urban areas. Even in its most expansive phase housebuilding investment was unable to keep pace with population increase [Wohl, 1977, *2*]. Housebuilding investment receded in the 1830s and plummeted in the 1840s [Cooney, 1980, *146*]. The flotation of railway shares severely dented the volume of funds available for residential construction, and after the late 1830s, with the exception of the mid-

18

Table 3   Housebuilding Investment 1760–1913

Decade	Housebuilding as % of GDFCF*	Decade	Housebuilding as % of GDFCF*
1761–70	22.4	1841–50	15.4
1771–80	19.6	1851–60	17.7
1781–90	19.5	1861–70	16.5
1791–1800	23.4	1871–80	20.3
1801–10	27.6	1881–90	18.1
1811–20	28.4	1891–1900	19.5
1821–30	31.5	1901–13	17.4
1831–40	26.6		

*GDFCF = Gross Domestic Fixed Capital Formation

Source: [Feinstein, 1978, *40*; 1972, *T88–9*]

1870s and late-1890s booms, housebuilding never again regained its late-eighteenth-century share of capital formation. As a result of these patterns of residential investment, the proportion of national wealth devoted to housing the nation diminished in the century before 1860, residential (and social) capital falling from 31 per cent of national wealth in 1760 to a plateau of 28 per cent 1800–30, and declining further by 1860 so that it accounted for only 24 per cent of national capital assets [Feinstein, 1978, *Table 27C*].

(b) Building costs and technology

Unlike thrusting technical advances in textiles, metallurgy and other sectors of nineteenth-century British industry, building technology remained virtually stagnant throughout the century, save for limited areas such as factory brick production and distribution, steam-powered wood dressing, and some reorganisation of on-site work preparation [Bowley, 1960, *61, 71*; Cooney, 1980, *150*; Price, 1980, *20*]. Consequently building costs remained stubbornly opposed to significant long-run price falls experienced by industrial products. From 1760 to 1800 building prices had risen faster, and between 1815 and 1850 had fallen less decisively, than general prices, and in conjunction with duties on timber, bricks, tiles, slate, and stone – which could add

19

50 per cent to the cost of a small house – and a window tax until 1851, housebuilding failed to extend potential demand as had other industries [Cooney, 1980, *110*; Burnett, 1978, *21*; Feinstein, 1978, *38*]. Some building materials (timber, stone, tiles, bricks) increased in price between 1845 and 1914, but others (glass, paint, lead, cement) fell, the net effect being a decline of about 30 per cent overall [Maiwald, 1954, *192*]. But this was almost exactly offset by rising labour costs [Powell, 1980, *75*] so that though short-term fluctuations continued, long-run building costs remained roughly stable in money terms. Proportionately rising labour costs diminished builders' entrepreneurial independence and contributed to a heightened tension in industrial relations after 1860 [McKenna and Rodger, 1985, *210*].

The real cost of housing space consistently increased relative to general prices. During the late eighteenth century building costs rose by 6 per cent more, and in the Napoleonic era by 40 per cent more than general prices; in the 1820–50 years building costs moved adversely by 19 per cent; and between 1850 and 1914 the stability of building costs meant a net disadvantage of 21 per cent compared to general price trends. Over the century and a half, decennial changes in building costs increased by 81 per cent; general prices, by contrast, fell by approximately 4 per cent over the same period. The real purchasing power for housing therefore was dramatically, if not evenly, eroded in comparison to the consumption of industrial products and foodstuffs, and in no years was this more pronounced than in the formative years of urban expansion before 1850.

(c) Building firms and organisational structure

Little ambiguity exists about the size of building industry firms. Irrespective of geographical location the small firm numerically continued to dominate the industry. Between 1779 and 1801, 85 per cent of Nottingham builders undertook only one project, and none more than three [Chalklin, 1976, *232*]. In 1851, 50 per cent of London builders and 94 per cent of joinery firms engaged fewer than ten workers [Jones, 1971, *374*], a pattern replicated in the English regions and Scottish burghs. In the second half of the century 70 per cent of Leicester housebuilding was undertaken in projects of five or fewer houses, and in thirty Scottish burghs 54 per cent of projects were for building a single house [Pritchard, 1976, *39*; Rodger, 1976, *228*]. During 1865–1900, 50 per cent of Sheffield builders put up no more than three houses, and 75 per cent built eight or fewer houses [Aspinall, 1982, *94*]. Though small firms remained most numerous, there were some giant undertakings. Three of the five firms with more than 350 employees in 1851 were London-based, and nine out of nineteen firms with 200 or more employees were also in the capital [Cooney, 1980, *157*]. By 1873, six London builders each engaged more than 800 workers, 41 had 200 or more, and this was part of a gradual national trend towards larger building firms from the 1870s [Dyos, 1961, *124*; 1968, *653*].

An earlier organisational change in the building industry occurred around 1790 when general contracting was added to the three traditional types of building firm [Cooney, 1955, *167*]. These three were, firstly, master craftsmen who worked only at their trades, engaging a few journeymen; secondly, master craftsmen responsible for an entire building who, though directly employing labour in their specialist area, subcontracted other work; thirdly, a builder who though not himself a craftsman, undertook buildings based on a series of contracts with craftsmen. Employers such as Thomas Cubitt and Alexander Copland (London), John Carter (Nottingham), Richard Kendall and Richard Paley (Leeds) with a permanent workforce in all crafts represented a new departure in building organisation at the dawn of the century. Not only were larger projects feasible through general contracting, but speculative ones were essential to ensure full utilisation of the greater capital and labour resources involved [Price, 1980, *23*]. The importance of continuity in building work to cash flow required such 'master builders' to embark upon speculative housebuilding in between contract building and what had commenced as a business expedient became a central strategy as builders recognised that previously occasional opportunities to anticipate demand were a permanent feature in the context of continuing population growth and urbanisation. Such conditions applied most conspicuously in London, Lancashire, and other northern and midland towns, and by 1825 general

21

contracting was established there, boosted further in the 1830s by railway construction. Speculative housebuilding, therefore, originally a business convenience, assumed unprecedented proportions not only as general contracting gained strength but as small firms emulated their larger brethren, so much so that by the 1870s 90 per cent of Camberwell was constructed speculatively [Dyos, 1961, *125*].

The widespread emergence of speculative builders in early-nineteenth-century decades was an organisational response to redefined market opportunities. It polarised the building industry between speculative and contract builders, between opportunist profit takers and those with long-term commitment to the industry. It introduced work control practices on site, initiated a new phase of industrial relations, and most important, intensified instability [Price, 1980, *26*]. Speculative housebuilders introduced a more dynamic mode of organisation, analogous to factory production, and jeopardised an element of stability derived from craft producers, replacing it with aggressive competition, unsold houses, risk and uncertainty [McKenna and Rodger, 1985, *208*]. As a result, building fluctuations between 1890 and 1913 were 70 per cent more pronounced than those in manufacturing industry. Accommodating such variations required a fineness of business judgement beyond many builders and bankruptcy was commonplace [Powell, 1986, *65*]. Judging future household formation through changes in marriage rates and local employment prospects was itself problematical; adjusting housebuilding was in the short term virtually impossible as builders needed to complete dwellings to sell, and thus repay loans on them [Lewis, 1965, *218*]. This tendency for housing completions to continue long after demand had peaked caused a saturation of the market which itself could take eight or more years to eliminate, with new building meanwhile almost non-existent. Thus few Camberwell firms of the 1850s survived into the 1870s, and the collapse of the City of Glasgow Bank in 1878 so exposed the tenuous basis of west of Scotland builders that two-thirds of them went bankrupt. Housing quality suffered in this volatile climate, since builders skimped to maximise profits, paid low wages for substandard work, and used inferior materials in an effort to cut costs. The widespread use by the 1830s of the term 'jerry-builder', denoting the temporary nature of many dwellings, was an explicit acknowledgement of such practices.

(d) Building finance

For large and small building firms alike, sources of capital were almost invariably local and heavily dependent on personal contact; throughout the nineteenth century bank finance, limited liability, and stock market quotation were exceptional [Dyos, 1968, *644*]. Most builders depended on a mixture of financial sources – trade credit from materials suppliers, cash advances from customers, loans obtained by issuing a bond on security of houses to be erected on future ground rents, and past profits.

For houses built by agreement customers themselves made lump sum advances to housebuilders, often proportionate to the extent of building progress. Many were erected in pairs, with shopkeepers, clerks and skilled labourers advancing cash for such projects, in one of which they would themselves reside, letting the adjacent house for a rental income [Crossick, 1983, *319*]. Private savings often financed middle-class housing, though estate developers were also involved in funding street layout, utilities, and the houses themselves. Later in the century, railway, mining and shipbuilding companies became significant localised housebuilders, as they sought to secure a stable workforce, and from the 1890s local authorities directly or through subcontracting intervened to build council housing. In each case builders obtained a measure of assurance as regards financial advances and final sale [Powell, 1980, *49*].

The same might be said of another tier of finance – building societies. Concentrated in midland and northern towns, about 250 societies were formed in the half century following the first in 1775 [Dyos, 1961, *114*]. They were petit bourgeois and artisanal extensions of collecting clubs. Regular subscriptions financed housebuilding for the membership, lots being drawn to establish the order by which subscribers took possession of completed houses [Chapman and Bartlett, 1971, *236*]. Detailed rules and procedures governed the societies, the majority of which until the last quarter of the nineteenth century were terminating, that is, concluded upon the completion of mem-

23

bers' housing, a process taking normally about ten years [Rimmer, 1963, *309*]. For thirty years after 1800 an average of 100 societies was formed annually, a rate of growth which necessitated clarification of legal status (1812) and a measure of legislative supervision (1836). Formalised control and legal status further boosted development so that during the 1850s and 1860s approximately 1500–2000 societies were active at any one time, two-thirds of them in Lancashire, the West Riding, Staffordshire, and Middlesex [Cleary, 1965, *26, 287*]. In national terms, building clubs probably financed about 12–15 per cent of houses by the 1860s, more in their northern strongholds, and as much as 25 per cent of housing in South Wales by 1914 [Daunton, 1983, *196*]. These early-nineteenth-century mutual societies established regional traditions of owner occupancy, conspicuously absent, for example, in Scottish burghs, and though statutorily regulated from 1874 and reorganised in 1894, it was not until after the First World War that national building societies came to dominate the mortgage market.

Assured financial sources were beyond the reach of the majority of builders for whom a facility to raise and renegotiate loans was critical. Many looked no further than family, friends and trade associates, while others developed a systematic network of contacts from whom loans were regularly obtained [Crossick, 1983, *389*]. In this, the legal profession was conspicuously active, channelling trust funds, marriage settlements, and widows' inheritances into housing [Chalklin, 1976, *239*; Rodger, 1979, *230*]. A dependable, if unspectacular, investment income was sought by solicitors on their clients' behalf, either as fixed term loans to builders or as cash advances towards housing for rental income. Not only were solicitors instrumental in directing loans towards the property sector, they too, like other professionals and manufacturers, were active on their own account. When aged about 40 to 50, this social group sought incomes from predictable property investment rather than from higher risk securities as the basis for their incomes in old age [Morris, 1979, *110*; 1983, *295*]. Thus, lawyers and locally known individual lenders considerably deepened the reservoir of available private mortgages and building finance [Elliott and McCrone, 1980, *10*].

Whereas the emergent building societies lent money on a

24

fixed long-term basis during which time the principal and interest was repaid, privately arranged mortgages could be recalled at any time and with the principal repaid in full [Rodger, 1979, *233*]. This was the central attraction to the lender: full repayment at short notice, collateral in the form of buildings in case of default, and an interest rate normally 1 per cent above consols. To borrowers, delaying repayments avoided a drain on working capital and provided flexibility over whether and when to renegotiate a loan, options unavailable with building society mortgages. Privately arranged loans afforded advantages to both lenders and borrowers so long as the property market was in some measure of equilibrium. But borrowing on short term against a product completed and sold over a much longer period meant builders were vulnerable to investors' changing perceptions of property prospects. An inability to renegotiate loans on call or at maturity caused an abrupt cessation to building and led inexorably to bankruptcy for small and speculative builders for whom completion, sale and repayment provided the lifeline to continuity in the industry. Simultaneous defaults by a number of local builders brought a full-scale crisis of confidence, further calls for loan repayment, and a renewed bout of bankruptcies amongst builders, not to mention a legacy of distrust and unsold houses which took several years to eradicate [Cairncross, 1953, *31*]. When, in 1915, the government prevented lenders' entitlement to recall loans at short notice it officially acknowledged the importance of raising and renegotiating loans as the most important of builders' survival skills, and one which in the climate of acute uncertainty and instability had had a prejudicial impact on the quality and quantity of Victorian housing.

The systematic development of ground rents offered another opportunity to raise finance [Dyos, 1961, *88*]. A builder or developer could create ground rents, a small annual charge on each building plot, sufficient to cover his own ground rent obligations and obtain a surplus. Capitalised on the strength of future income, this provided a cash advance to commence building. For example, an acre of land purchased or leased with an annual ground rent burden of £60 could be recovered by developing an estate of 25 houses, each paying £5 to provide a gross revenue of £125. The annual surplus, £65, and the entitlement to it could be sold, perhaps at 20 years purchase, to provide a capital sum of £1300 with which to commence building operations. Variants of this strategy existed, and though not geographically widespread, were an accepted tactic in Scotland [Rodger, 1983, *202*]. As a result, some small builders obtained disproportionate capital sums for a very modest down payment on a plot of land.

With the exception of building societies, these various sources of finance changed very little in the course of the nineteenth century. With no professional barriers on who undertook building and ineffectual monitoring of housing standards before 1858, the nature of the supply of capital encouraged heavy participation by small and speculative building firms. While good-quality housing was less affected, these features of the building industry left an indelible mark on low-income housing. Many streets took years to complete and inferior materials and workmanship produced a stock of damp, insanitary and pestilential houses as builders sought to escape the clutches of the receiver by maximising short-term profits in the upswing phase of the cycle without much regard for housing quality and long-term stability in the building industry.

(iii) THE CONTAINING CONTEXT: BUILDING REGULATIONS

Between 1800 and 1845 almost 400 Local Improvement Acts covering building regulation and sanitary control in 208 English and Welsh towns were approved by Parliament. Such feverish legislative activity confirmed the urgency of the housing problem yet it did little to reverse the structural and sanitary shortcomings of housing [Gaskell, 1983, *6*; Harper, 1985, *xv*; Tarn, 1973, *7*]. Quite simply this was because of lax drafting, unenforceable clauses, ineffectual monitoring, jurisdictional limitations, regulatory exclusion of existing housing, and administrative responsibility fragmented amongst several vestries, parishes and town councils within the urban area. So, despite increasingly convincing early-Victorian statistical evidence linking mortality, sanitary and housing conditions, effective municipal intervention to regulate building remained on the horizon, and was opposed by prevailing *laissez-faire* thinking, the vested interests of local builders and the sanctity of private property rights. More specifically, there was force in contemporaries' arguments that building bye-laws increased housing costs so that in protecting consumers' interests in respect of the quality of space, they could actually afford less of it, a persistent dilemma throughout the century [Beresford, 1971, *112*].

The reform of local government under the Municipal Corporations Act (1835) paved the way for individual boroughs to initiate tougher building codes. In general, the preference for jealously guarded local autonomy inclined councils to obtain appropriate powers by selectively drawing on national legislation or through Local Improvement Acts as in Leeds where, after 1842, new housing had compulsorily to be connected to sewers or cesspools. Though Newcastle (1837), Leeds and Liverpool (1842), anticipated the Metropolitan Building Act (1844) in London, and were closely followed by Manchester (1845), the introduction of local bye-laws stipulating wall thicknesses and minimum street width offered only partial and rudimentary codes; achievements were modest when confrontted with the pace of urban growth and building development [Wohl, 1983, *309*]. Adoptive, rather than mandatory, legislation proved largely ineffectual. For example, the Public Health Act 1848 provisions for drains, water supply, street paving and cleansing gave broad scope for continuing abuse, and in 1858, the newly constituted Local Government Office, conscious of environmental needs but also of the delicate tension between central and local government, tentatively suggested a 'Form of Bye-laws', national guidelines for building regulations which would be locally applied [Gaskell, 1983, *21*]. So by the 1860s the combination of adoptive national statutes and local Acts, though important in terms of legislative development, had barely addressed the housing problem; as long as builders vaguely observed elementary fire and safety codes, sanitary and structural regulations could be disregarded (see p. 48). In general they were, and the irregular, congested, insanitary 'rookeries' resulted, a combined product of demand and supply forces operating in a vacuum of environmental control.

4 House Types: Terraces and Tenements

(i) RESIDENTIAL SEGREGATION AND MOBILITY

Urban population growth and the low wages underpinning nineteenth-century industrialisation combined with the characteristics of landowning and building to produce high-density housing. This economic equation created a hierarchical division of society based increasingly on income differentials, with numerous and narrowly spaced rungs on the social ladder translated into distinctions in house form [Conzen, 1981, *117*]. So if the Georgian terrace became the generic house type in nineteenth-century England, vernacular versions reflected these hierarchical social divisions [Muthesius, 1982, *237*]. Ornamentation and internal accommodation became an explicit proclamation of status. While income gradations between skilled and unskilled, clerks and the middle class existed, similarities within each socio-economic subgroup, defined by ideals and cultural values, were given greater coherence by virtue of residential proximity [Pooley, 1979, *275*]. During the nineteenth century the pre-industrial residential mix was increasingly abandoned in favour of more carefully delineated areas of homogeneous housing, a process eventually accelerated by standardised building regulations [Daunton, 1983, *7*], but introduced by developers and builders as a convenience in constructing uniform streets. Standardisation cut costs and reduced rents. Each additional feature – a third bedroom or a kitchen range – added costs, increased rents and filtered out successive income groups. In general, affordability determined exclusivity. The mechanism was no less applicable to working-class neighbourhoods than to high-class suburbia.

This filtration process based on affordable rents was under way in late-Georgian Britain [Laxton, 1980, *87*]; by 1850 the tendency towards residential segregation was well established.

Though closely identified with the process of suburbanisation, segregation was not confined to the middle class or large cities, and did not always produce homogeneous or single-class areas since complex social alliances on ethnic, religious, workplace and other bases were superimposed upon residential patterns determined by income level and the ability to pay rent [Dennis, 1984, *215, 247*; Gordon, 1979, *170*; Carter and Wheatley, 1982, *78, 110*; Cowlard, 1979, *243*]. How far new socially and residentially distinct areas emerged with a definite sense of community and neighbourhood is difficult to assess and complicated by the frequent relocation of households. Victorians moved often, normally over short distances and within range of family and community support networks, especially retail credit, church and interest groups [Pritchard, 1976, *57*]. Glasgow landlords (1900) reckoned 5–6 months as the average tenancy [Englander, 1983, *8*], and in Liverpool (1851, 1871) 40 per cent of the population moved house within one year and 50 per cent within two years [Dennis, 1984, *257*]. After 12 months, 20–25 per cent of households in York in 1844, Manchester in 1868, Leicester in 1870–1 and Cardiff in the 1880s had changed address; after two years, 35–44 per cent had moved. Address changes were less frequent amongst the middle classes, older age groups and locally born compared to the unskilled, unmarried, newly wed and migrants [Pooley, 1979, *267*]. That address changes were also less frequent in expanding compared to declining industrial centres, for example in St Helens rather than Wigan, and in manufacturing towns with diversified economic structures rather than seaports [Jackson, 1981, *427*] has confirmed skill and continuity of employment and earnings as crucial to residential persistence and the development of a community identity [Foster, 1977, *106*].

(ii) EVOLUTION OF THE TERRACED HOUSE

From the irregular street pattern and frontages of pre-modern towns the geometric regularity of Victorian terraced housing seems far removed. Yet the two were interlinked. The rectilineal patterns induced by building bye-laws (1858, 1875) were clearly not the formative influence, and though terraced housing owed some parentage to a mimicry of high-status Georgian terrace architecture [Muthesius, 1982, *16*], three further influences can be traced [Rimmer, 1963, *180*; Beresford, 1971, *98*; Chapman, 1971, *140, 224*]. Firstly, a type of ribbon development spread rapidly outwards along transport routes from expanding eighteenth-century towns and this roadside parallelism produced an embryonic terrace more regular than previous street alignments. Secondly, infill housing was constructed in numerous existing shop and inn yards, town house gardens and orchards where narrow burgage frontages disguised extensive back lands. Lining the interior walls of a garden with cottages permitted rapid parallel additions to the housing stock at no great distance from the workplace, and when adjacent courtyards with a shared boundary wall were also lined with new housing the transition to back-to-back housing was almost inadvertent. Sufficient land behind the principal thoroughfares enabled the eighteenth-century population increase to be accommodated without recourse to town extensions. Continued pressure required entirely new settlements and terraced housing proved acceptable because of earlier familiarity, because low-cost alternatives such as cellar accommodation were regarded as inferior, and because terrace design was validated as a vernacular echo of fashionable architectural style. Thirdly, when urban sprawl eventually absorbed green-field sites developers quickly recognised that maximising rentals or the sale of building plots was consistent with a grid-iron lay-out which easily matched the original field shape [Conzen, 1981, *115*]. Fitting straight lines of housing into former rectangular fields maximised the built-up area, coincided with the market dictates of containing costs and rents, and simplified the building process because of stereotyped plans, simple levels and straight lines each of which enhanced labour productivity because of familiar work routines.

(iii) THE HOUSING HIERARCHY

Ill-ventilated housing attracted vehement condemnation in Victorian Britain. This was because until the 1870s, when general acceptance of the transmission of disease by water-borne

30

organisms so transformed attitudes to domestic water-supply and sanitation, contamination from air-borne sources – the 'miasmic' theory – remained uppermost [Wohl, 1983, *89*]. Preoccupation with the physical structure of and spatial arrangements within houses consequently governed contemporaries' approaches towards early reform measures.

(a) Common lodging houses

For migrants to the city without kinship support to provide temporary housing, common lodging houses offered a bed for a few pence per night. Intended originally as short-term housing for men, common lodging houses evolved as long-term hostel accommodation, often for families, which with their communal living and dormitory sleeping arrangements proved offensive to Victorian values [Chapman, 1971, *82*]. Double cellars, flatted tenements and even terraced housing served as common lodging houses. At a conservative estimate, London in 1854 had officially 10,824 common lodging houses with 82,000 residents nightly [Wohl, 1977, *74*]; in a 440-yard semicircle from Leeds parish church 222 lodging houses accommodated 2500 people at an average of 2.5 persons per bed and 4.5 persons per room [Burnett, 1978, *60*]. Such overcrowding nurtured epidemic disease, but equally alarming to contemporaries was the exposure of children to immorality and criminality which, despite perfectly respectable examples of lodging houses, lingered in the public perception as an unacceptable institutionalisation of vice, and therefore the target of early, if ineffective, legislative control from 1851 [Gauldie, 1974, *242*].

(b) Cellar dwellings

With a floor area commonly 12ft × 12ft, ceilings of 6ft, and mostly without windows or flagged floors, cellars were predictably dark, damp and disease-ridden [Burnett, 1978, *60*]. Some were below shops and warehouses, others in more generous middle-class basements, but the majority were beneath terraced housing. Though relatively scarce in Birmingham and Nottingham, 3 per cent of the Leeds population in 1840, 12–15 per cent in Manchester, and approximately 20 per cent in Liverpool inhabited cellars [Rimmer, 1963, *181*; Dennis, 1984, *60*].

31

Without solid floors damp was a constant problem. Sanitation was totally lacking. All refuse had to be removed through a single door. Unable to rent anything better, migrants, the poor and destitute were obliged to inhabit such cellar or lodging house accommodation, the lowest echelons of the housing hierarchy [Taylor, 1970, *73*].

(c) Terraced housing

(i) Back-to-back and court housing.   According to the Registrar General's 1839 report, 'the rate of mortality depends upon the efficiency of the ventilation [and on] the removal of impurities'.[9] These shortcomings were particularly apparent in court and terraced housing at the lower end of the rental spectrum. High-density terraced housing with a common back wall (i.e. back-to-back) was transplanted from its late-eighteenth-century infancy to full maturity in the early nineteenth century. This deliberate attempt to pack as many houses as possible on a limited site was most effectively achieved by eliminating streets so that acres of terraced housing were accessible only by a series of narrow alleys or passages (see Figure 2). Identical rows each of 6–10 back-to-back houses were erected 9–15 ft apart. These inward-looking courts were closed at both ends either by a block of communal privies and ashpits, or by another terrace of houses. A 4 ft wide and 3–5 ft high covered gap or tunnel in the lines of terraced houses allowed entry to the court beyond where the pattern was exactly replicated [Muthesius, 1982, *106*]. Courts reached their zenith in the 1840s when in Liverpool 25 per cent of the population was housed in this manner. Despite problems of quantification, back-to-back housing including courts constituted about 65–70 per cent of the total housing stock in Birmingham, Nottingham, Liverpool and other northern and midland strongholds in the 1840s, and continued at about the 70 per cent level in Leeds, Huddersfield, Keighley and other West Riding towns until the 1880s [Burnett, 1978, *74*]. Between 12 and 20 per cent of Belfast housing in 1851 was in the form of back-to-backs in 1851;[10] and they were also a significant proportion of the housing stock in south London, Stepney, Mile End, and not uncommon in the boroughs of southern England [Wohl, 1977, *135*].

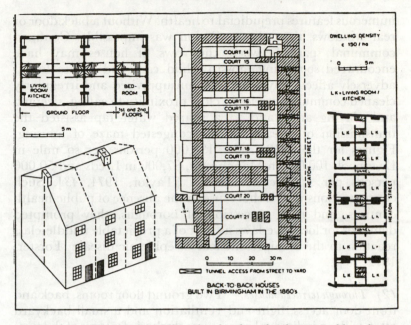

Figure 2   Typical mid-Victorian back-to-back terraced housing

The internal plan of the back-to-back house was very simple. A living room 10–15 ft square was entered directly from the court or street. Dark, narrow stairs led to another room of identical dimensions. This one-up, one-down 'single-pile' house 'was the most frequent type until the middle of the century', though in Leicester, Nottingham, London and Liverpool, indeed in most older cities, a further attic workroom/bedroom was common, as was a sublet cellar. Local variants in access gave an idiosyncratic character to court housing in Hull and Rochdale, while steep hillsides in Burnley, Halifax and Pennine towns generally produced local nuances in the terraced housing [Caffyn, 1986; Muthesius, 1982, *101*]. Regional building customs and local preferences [Beresford, 1971, *126*] may explain the finer variations but the undoubted dominance of the terraced form confirms that the architectural resolution of the demand and supply equation was broadly the same throughout England and Wales.

Internally and externally back-to-back housing exhibited

numerous features prejudicial to health. Without a back door or rear windows, through ventilation was impossible. Confined communal space between the rows of houses may have encouraged socialising, gossip, child care and games but it adversely affected hygiene since unsupervised and irregularly cleaned communal privies in close proximity to eating, sleeping and playing areas and to a shared water tap assisted the transmission of diseases in the congested maze of housing. Figures for the 1840s show 138,000 persons per sq. mile in Liverpool, 100,000 in Manchester, 87,000 in Leeds and 50,000 persons per sq. mile in London [Taylor, 1974, *43*]. Such concentrations were a short fuse in the absence of public health controls, and in a succession of boroughs, they prompted demands for local bye-laws as part of a predictable middle-class reaction to the omnipresent fear of epidemic disease [Forster, 1972, *28*].

(2) Through terraced houses. Two ground floor rooms, back and front door access, light and ventilation and a small backyard often with an individual privy were the basic features of the two-up, two-down terraced house (see Figure 3). More space meant greater possibilities for privacy and separation of cooking, living and sleeping areas. A front downstairs room, the 'parlour', was commonly retained for 'ceremonial' use: entertaining visitors, family celebrations and wakes. In the second half of the nineteenth century further functional specialisation of rooms was made possible, firstly by a rear annex, a one-storey addition which provided a scullery with a sink and boiler, a coal house and a WC; secondly, by an additional storey to the rear annex to add a third bedroom; and thirdly, by widening the house frontage to allow entry from the street into a hallway rather than directly into the front room. Such amenities added to building costs; rentals reflected this so that the housing hierarchy was in reality a rental hierarchy with working-class segregation a function of income flows.

(d) Regional Housing Variants

(1) Tyneside flats. Two-storey terraced flats were the prevalent house type in a narrow riverside strip on either side of

34

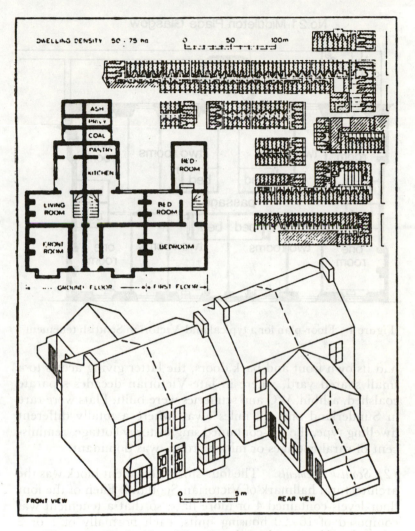

Figure 3   Typical late-Victorian through terraced housing

the Tyne [Muthesius, 1982, *130*]. In Newcastle, Gateshead and South Shields houses were crowded on the steep hillsides close to the river and a strong tendency for flatted housing developed, so much so that by 1911 almost two-thirds of Tyneside dwellings were flats [Daunton, 1983, *40*]. Distinctively private, each flat

35

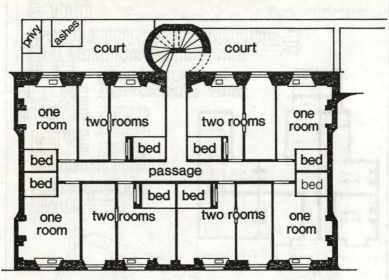

No.21 Middleton Place Glasgow

Figure 4   Floor-plan for a typical mid-Victorian Scottish tenement

had its own front and back doors, the latter giving access to a small shared yard, where in late-Victorian decades separate coalshed, ashbin, WC and sculleries were built. Flats were rare in Sunderland only 12 miles away where a totally different dwelling type, the self-contained single-storey cottage, reminiscent of rural cottages or miners' rows, was dominant.

(2) Scottish tenements.   The four-storey tenement block was the architectural hallmark of Victorian Scotland. Each of the four floor levels contained 4 or more flats, so that a tenement was composed of 16–20 housing units, each normally of 1 or 2 rooms. Figure 4 shows a typical 1850s Glasgow tenement, in this case with 34 separate flats and one outside dry closet for about 130 residents. The reasons for this distinctive housing form were an amalgam of higher Scottish building costs, a unique tenurial system, known as feuing, which increased land costs and ground burdens, a method of building finance for small builders based on the technicalities of feuing which intensified building industry instability, and average real wages approximately 20–

30 per cent below comparable English trades in the 1850s [Rodger, 1983, *211*; 1986, *153*]. To make matters worse, in the context of the Scottish system of yearly lettings, tenants chose a flat based on a rent affordable in the worst employment weeks of their working year, a necessarily cautious strategy from which a mean standard of accommodation resulted. This contrasted with short English tenancies which allowed greater flexibility in adjusting housing to changing incomes.

Faced with weak purchasing power and higher supply prices in the form of house rents, Scots could not participate in the English tradition, however basic, of self-contained terraced housing. Undifferentiated rooms meant food preparation and eating, sleeping, work, births and deaths, nursing and children's play all took place within the same areas, necessitating frequent inconvenient efforts to redefine floor space for each purpose. Block dwellings themselves imposed living conditions which adversely affected life expectancy and repressed physical development. Defective ventilation and darkness were ever present features, only intensified when further 60 ft-high blocks were built to the rear in a Scottish high rise equivalent of English courts described as 'an aggravated form of the back-to-back house' by a Glasgow Medical Officer of Health [Rodger, 1986, *158*]. Narrow interconnecting closes and wynds accentuated these shortcomings. External stairs were dangerous; internal ones dark, insanitary and a fire hazard. Water pumping and storage were expensive in tenements and this contrasted strongly with the ground level supplies available to English terraced houses. Until the 1880s therefore, WCs were usually located at ground level, one or at best two being shared by the entire tenement. Accordingly, overcrowded housing, defined as more than two persons per room, was extreme in Scotland; more than 70 per cent of residents in Coatbridge, Wishaw and Kilsyth lived in overcrowded conditions, and in nine further Strath-clyde burghs overcrowding rates of between 60 and 69 per cent were ten times those of Liverpool, Manchester or Hull in 1911. In the best-housed Scottish city, Edinburgh, overcrowding was equivalent to the worst English boroughs on Tyneside and in London's East End, and in Scotland nationally overcrowding (45 per cent) was five times greater than in England (9 per cent) in 1911.[11]

5 The Suburbs — Villas and Values

The years 1815–50 were ones of conscious suburbanisation. Deliberately, and for the first time, new and exclusively middle-class zones were created to provide socially intact areas in stark contrast to the residential mix typical of pre-industrial towns [Thompson, 1982, 7]. Architectural historians confirm that detached and semi-detached houses built for single family occupancy were the quintessential suburban type and that before 1794, when the Eyre estate (St John's Wood, London) was begun, virtually no such houses existed [Summerson, 1945, *158*; Olsen, 1976, *215*]. Before that date attempted suburban developments, for example in Liverpool (Toxteth Park) and Birmingham (Ashted) failed, and even Edgbaston proved problematical until, like Everton, sufficient numbers of the new manufacturing and mercantile bourgeoisie began to populate it in the 1820s [Chalklin, 1974, *110*; Cannadine, 1980, *91*].

The middle class were not a homogeneous group and suburbs were consequently differentiated to reflect social gradations. In addition to the Palladian or Gothic style country villas built in their own grounds, three principal types of suburb have been identified [Summerson, 1945, *255*; Tarn (Simpson and Lloyd), 1977, *175*]. Firstly, village developments a few miles from the city centre [Dulwich, Hampstead (London); Prestwich, Chorlton (Manchester); Gorbals, Partickhill (Glasgow); Chapeltown, Headingley (Leeds)]; secondly, ribbon developments encouraged by improved road surfaces for expanded turnpike traffic [Islington, Southwark, Camden (London); the Antrim and Dublin Roads (Belfast); Gosforth (Newcastle)]; and thirdly, estates planned by speculative builders frequently between main roads [Paddington, Somers Town (London); Sharrow, Broomhall (Sheffield), Clifton (Bristol); New Walk (Leicester)].

How can this new suburbanising trend, 1815–50, be explained? The simplest argument revolves on urban size, that beyond some threshold, perhaps around 50,000 people, achieved by individual cities at varying dates, the physical unity which integrated the social, political and economic activity of the town crumbled [Thompson, 1982, 5]. London conspicuously, but also Manchester, Glasgow, Liverpool, Birmingham and Bristol were already past the 50,000 mark in 1800; Leeds, Sheffield and Newcastle soon followed. In the early nineteenth century each spawned discrete middle-class suburbs. Urban scale, therefore, reached such proportions as to impose diseconomies – additional costs and time – which impeded business, social relations and communications. The city accordingly became more specialised or zoned, a process accelerated by railway development from the 1830s, with a central business district, workshop and residential areas. Suburbs, then, were partly a product of increasing urban size; in the wake of industrialisation the middle classes for the first time were sufficiently numerous to produce a coherent entity rather than being confined, as previously, to a few streets or squares.

Whether the building industry changed sufficiently in the 1820s to propel suburbanisation is doubtful. The termination of wartime conditions in 1815 assisted both a short-run decline in materials costs and eased building finance [Lewis, 1965, 31]. Building land on the urban fringe remained easily available, and if the emergence of general building contractors heralded an organisational change in the industry, it had not proceeded very far by the 1820s; nor was it exclusively associated with suburbanisation.

Were transport changes influential? Passenger networks required passengers to generate adequate revenue to operate. Consequently they followed rather than preceded residential development [Dennis, 1984, 110]. Short-stage coaches, already well developed in London in 1800, evolved into horse-drawn omnibuses by 1830, later in other cities, with more capacity, easy boarding and lower fares [Thompson, 1974, 55; Simpson, 1977, 45]. By their timing horse buses sustained but did not initiate the suburbanising process, though they did facilitate suburban colonisation adjacent to routes served by them. As with trams after 1870, the expectation was that transport services would soon follow suburban development. Railways influenced housing in central districts where access routes, stations and goods yards demolished properties and displaced residents, inflated land values and introduced physical barriers to mobility. But many companies opposed suburban passenger traffic especially if it was at cheap fares, and so in English cities, railways contributed little to suburbanisation [Kellett, 1969, *15, 337, 354*; Reeder, 1968, *268*].

How far architectural design created the suburb is debatable. Shaw's villas in St John's Wood (1790s) and Nash's Georgian terraces overlooking Regent's Park (1810s) were certainly appealing to the rustic aspirations of a population many of whom had recently migrated from rural areas.[12] Yet with middle-class preferences in Scotland loyal to tenement dwelling and an English middle class still often housed in terraces, rural influences on architecture were moderated by two other, arguably more powerful influences: a preference for privacy, and a trend towards individualism rather than communality. Both required more space between houses and neighbours [Olsen, 1976, *21, 213*].

Victorian values and in particular evangelical doctrine offered a vigorous stimulus to suburbanisation. Personal resurrection or rebirth underlay a view of individual salvation regarded as essential to counteract the social disorder of revolutionary France and the malaise of early-nineteenth-century British cities [Davidoff and Hall, 1987, *82*]. Such thinking underpinned the virtues of sobriety, thrift and cleanliness in relation to the home which was seen as having a strong moral purpose [Tarn, 1971, *1*]. Moral reform began with the basic unit of society, the family, in which the wife and mother was a decisive influence. (Simultaneously the family accorded her a lifetime role in a phase of shrinking middle-class employment options [Doe, 1976, *175*].) Based on a code which stressed domestic privacy, sexual separation, social distancing, and the cultivation of propriety, discipline and cleanliness, evangelical moral rearmament of the 1790s achieved a widespread acceptance in Anglican and Nonconformist circles by the 1830s [Davidoff and Hall, 1987, *180*]. The cult of privacy, therefore, rejected street and house arrangements where congestion, communality, noise and public access damaged self-discipline, extinguished self-sufficiency and, crucially, diminished parental responsibility. It was not simply the physical structures themselves which undermined decency and the family unit — there were many examples of generously proportioned and well-maintained terraced housing and tenement flats — it was the congestion with which they were associated. Values, not villas, preserved the residential unity which characterised the suburb.

Privacy and domesticity coincided with the emerging doctrine of 'separate spheres' since by the nature of increasing technical scale and complexity business organisation was inappropriately discharged from the home. The resulting separation of work and home isolated men from house and family, and though they retained economic dominance based on their workplace, the vacuum encouraged a female supremacy in the domestic arena [Davidoff, 1974, *364*]. This division was recognised and strengthened from the pulpit in an effort to stabilise middle-class moral values and in the expectation that they would then permeate other classes. How far the working class were willing accomplices in these family and domestic patterns and how far they were infiltrated by middle-class values for the purposes of social control and manipulation remains uncertain. What is clear is that later nineteenth-century housing at all levels became increasingly introspective, self-contained, and with this privatisation of domestic space, acquisitions of consumer goods and personal possessions were both possible and defensible, and gardening feasible [Doe, 1976, *177*; Daunton, 1983, *12*; Davidoff and Hall, 1987, *370*; Burnett, 1978, *193*].

Another line of explanation is to regard suburbs as the logical middle-class response to the intensifying death, disease and depravity thought to be products of the uncontrolled urban environment [Gauldie, 1974, *124*]. The filth and stench of the courts, yards and streets were offensive and hazardous to all and in the absence of early nineteenth-century administrative apparatus to control it, or engineering expertise to remove it, to flee from it made practical sense. The preference for hillside suburbs exposed to prevailing westerly winds uncontaminated by industrial and domestic pollutants was understandable in the light of statistical evidence and medical explanations which stressed air-borne contamination.

To explain suburbanisation merely as a response to public health dangers is an oversimplification. Indeed, middle-class economic power itself contributed to precisely those living conditions from which they fled by deriving a rentier income from slums, by reinvesting business profits to the exclusion of environmental improvement, and crucially, by diverting housing investment to the suburbs [Dyos and Reeder, 1973, *376*]. Suburbs were themselves the creation of capital, part of the ceaseless search for new investment outlets. Suburbs provided an integrated self-sustaining capitalist mechanism in pre-1850 years and beyond, by generating custom for property developers, suppliers of building materials, furnishers, for transport operators, retailing and entertainment interests, and by providing opportunities for water and gas companies, not to mention new outlets for lenders and landlords, and the professional activities of solicitors, bankers, savings institutions and others associated with property transactions. This 'bonanza' of new horizons for middle-class employment, profit and dividends was allied to further advantages. Suburbs gave access to the cheapest land to those with the greatest security of employment and with leisure to enjoy it. Suburbs also offered opportunities for the 'manipulation of social distinctions to those most aware of their possibilities and most adept at turning them into shapes on the ground'. Finally suburbs distanced the threat of social change. An 'ecological marvel', the suburb was a spatial device which inoculated the middle class against the hazards of the city without requiring them to relinquish their political control over it.

Suburbs were part of a process by which the middle classes developed institutions to control power and influence in the face of significant changes caused by industrialisation and urbanisation.[13] Peterloo (1819), the Merthyr Rising (1831), emergent trade unionism and other expressions of class tension could be controlled by cultural and residential unity in the suburbs, an embattled response, or by manipulation of urban institutions such as the town council and law enforcement through the instruments of legitimate political power, the ballot box, or by the management of informal networks, through professional bodies and employers' associations, or by a combination of these methods [Morris, 1983, *298*; Davidoff and Hall, 1987, *416*]. Suburbs and the suburbans were, therefore, a consciously developed cog in the mechanism for maintaining, consolidating and defending political power and the Great Reform Bill (1832)

42

and municipal reform (1834/5) only recognised a process already under way by 1830 and which continued thereafter.

The tension between slum and suburb can be viewed as a deliberate perpetuation of the status quo in social relations through the mechanism of low wages [Castells, 1977, 263]. Profits were reinvested with a view to deriving productivity gains and further profits, a process dependent upon low-priced labour abundantly replenished by natural increase and urban immigration [Dyos, 1968, 27]. Capital accumulation and reinvestment therefore neglected environmental improvement unless it directly impaired workers' health and efficiency and landlords' rental incomes [Foster, 1977, 103]. The workforce was too poor and employers unwilling to consider substantive improvements. Viewed thus, capitalist accumulation generated two crises in the urban scene. One was the deterioration of significant portions of the capital stock, to which suburbs contributed and from which cities never recovered; the second was the creation of homogeneous inner city neighbourhoods in which working-class consciousness ultimately ran counter to capitalist interests. In these senses suburbs created inherent weaknesses in the control of cities which they were designed to perpetuate [Rose, 1981, 359].

6 The Containment of 'The Housing Problem' 1850–1880

Opposing views impeded substantial working-class housing progress until the last quarter of the nineteenth century. One view, advanced by Chadwick and early public health reformers, was that until urban drainage and water systems were improved then the morbid effects of insanitary housing would continue to imperil inhabitants' lives [Lambert, 1963, 50]. Factors external to the house – paving, street cleansing, sewers, drainage, water supply – were stressed as indispensable to environmental improvement and indissolubly linked to housing conditions, poverty and health. This view, penetrating but premature, was itself contaminated by association with Chadwick, his political antagonisms and administrative isolation. But it also foundered on its requirement for a quantum leap in public expenditure during the infancy of reformed local government sensitive to electors' parsimony [Hennock, 1963, 215]. So the alternative explanation prevailed: character deficiencies were responsible for the slums and so moral regeneration offered a solution to the housing problem [Wohl, 1977, 8, 50]. Influential popular literature sustained the view that criminal and Irish elements were a cancerous influence on normal working-class behaviour. The pig made the sty and not the sty the pig and so reform emphasised moral rather than environmental improvement, a stance which dovetailed with ideological strands such as Christian teaching regarding family life and sobriety, the sanctity of property rights, prevailing *laissez-faire* orthodoxy in economic and social affairs, and ratepayers' insistence on economism in government. This quartet of attitudes governed a defensive, minimalist posture towards housing problems for most of the century.

If homes rather than houses, moral reform rather than the supply of bricks and mortar, were the pivots of middle-class

44

housing initiatives the inconsistency of the moral offensive was evident in 1851 when the religious census recorded less than 50 per cent church attendance in the majority of English boroughs, a significant overestimate amongst the working class in inner city parishes who were the principal target of the sermonising [Dennis, 1984, *30*]. So from mid century, sensitised by streams of statistics, innumerable tracts from women charity workers and compelling accounts of housing conditions from Mayhew, Kingsley and a growing corps of medical and voluntary visitors, the underlying moral campaign was occasionally superseded by pragmatic initiatives, philanthropic and legislative, designed to ameliorate the most offensive housing conditions.

AGENCIES OF RESTRAINT ON HOUSING CONDITIONS

(a) Philanthropic capitalism

Exhortations from the pulpit and in editorial columns assumed a tangible expression in the model dwellings movement which engaged the housing problem on two fronts: commercial viability and alternative housing prototypes [Tarn, 1971, *10*]. Block buildings were intended models to both builders and tenants, demonstrating that a sufficient profit was feasible from working-class housing while also encouraging tenants to adopt habits conducive to decent living. Two pioneering organisations in this campaign which in London involved 30 model associations in the second half of the century, were the Metropolitan Association for Improving the Dwellings of the Industrious Classes (1841) and the Society for Improving the Condition of the Labouring Classes (SICLC) (1844) [Wohl, 1977, *146*]. Their creativity in block and cottage design was modest [Gaskell, 1986, *140*], and royal patronage and prestigious architects were insufficient to counteract the disincentives both to investors, because of an unacceptably low yield, and to tenants, as rents were too high for all but artisans. By the mid 1850s the SICLC was dormant; a decade later the Metropolitan Association had virtually ceased to build. Neither had built many dwellings – 1122 families housed by the Metropolitan and 453 families plus 200 single men by the SICLC in 1875. Both were principally London organisations, though the Metropolitan formed branches during the 1850s in Dudley, Bristol, Liverpool, Torquay, and a number of independent associations had followed their example, for example, in Wolverhampton, Nottingham, Halifax, Dublin [Tarn, 1973, 32; Daly, 1984, 295].

Reinvigorated in the 1860s by the formation of the Peabody Trust (1862), Improved Industrial Dwellings Company (1863), and the Artizans', Labourers' and General Dwellings Company (1867) as a result of the benefaction and personal commitment of, respectively, George Peabody, Sydney Waterlow and William Austin, these organisations counterpoised a 5 per cent commerical return with sound sanitary standards as a viable blueprint for private builders. Though £6.5m had been invested in the London model dwellings movement by 1885, a considerable transfer of wealth, and 29,700 families (147,000 people) rehoused on 54 sites, there was little indication that private builders and investors were attracted to model housing solutions. Residents' reactions to the intimidating institutional monotony strengthened preferences for terraces and villas while also stigmatising block designs later adopted by municipal housing [Gaskell (Sutcliffe) 1974, 114].

Philanthropic efforts were also directed towards existing housing conditions. Middle-class women visitors and 'bible-women' of all classes extolled the virtues of thrift, abstinence, dietetics, and moral standards, but dealt only with the symptoms of housing deficiencies [Summers, 1979, 51]. The causes of bad housing, according to Octavia Hill, were the product of two forces: the character and habits of tenants, and the conduct and values of landlords. Hill's housing management attempted to fuse Christian ethics with improved tenant-landlord relations for a social class below that catered for by model dwellings associations [Tarn, 1973, 14]. Hill opposed charity and impersonal block dwellings, stressed self-help, cleanliness and respectability, and insisted on regular rent payments and a system of personal visits to tenants from her co-workers which transformed the tension of landlord and tenant to something approaching supportive friendship [Gauldie, 1974, 213; Wohl, 1977, 179]. The London initiatives of Octavia Hill were adopted by her disciples and paralleled in other cities, for example Dublin,

46

Dundee and Manchester, but their impact was minor in relation to the scale of the housing problem, though it did propose an optimistic solution without significant redistribution of resources [Checkland, 1975, *319*].

Faced with high land costs in London and directed at an artisan stratum which could reasonably fend for itself, philanthropic initiatives *c.* 1845–80 were quantitatively insignificant in the context of overall housing needs [Ashworth, 1954, *84*]. The model dwellings phase did identify, if it did not resolve, problems of site costs, acquisition, and compensation to landlords which proved influential to ensuing municipal slum clearance initiatives [Yelling, 1986, *16*]. Whether by intervening in the housing market, philanthropy redefined *laissez-faire* attitudes [Tarn, 1973, *16*] is highly doubtful. Arguably it buttressed existing ideology, superimposing middle-class emphases on private property and repayment of debts upon a working-class preference for communality and neighbourliness. Philanthropic efforts also stigmatised sections of society according to who was acceptable to housing managers, thereby underscoring rather than redefining the Victorian distinction between the deserving and undeserving. For these reasons and because of the presumption that the building industry was still prepared to house the working class, philanthropic efforts demonstrate a continuity of ideology. In the longer term they also showed that successful businessmen and devoted housing managers could not reliably squeeze a modest return from building and house ownership, and so raised a question mark over the abilities of lesser mortals, private builders and landlords, to do so. Model dwellings and moral encouragement therefore were a marginal social experiment, delaying radical approaches to the housing problem, though without their prior elimination as a potential solution acceptance of municipal intervention would have proved ideologically more difficult.

(b) Company housing

The 1833 Factory Commission reported[14] that 168 out of 881 large firms (19 per cent) provided some housing for their workers as part of their need to attract labour to remote locations. Like earlier factory villages at New Lanark, Styal and

Hyde, the mid-Victorian model housing schemes of Titus Salt (Saltaire, Bradford 1853), Edward Ackroyd (Ackroydon, Halifax 1861), Crossley (West Hill Park, Halifax 1863), Richardson (Bessbrook, N. Ireland 1846), Pim (Harold's Cross, Dublin), and Wilson (Bromborough, Cheshire 1853) provided some benefits to workers, but were conceived by employers as an integral part of factory discipline and labour supply [Ashworth, 1954, *126*]. Management motives also embraced a Christian desire to improve workers' living conditions, an influence more pronounced in the later company housing of Cadbury's Bournville (begun 1879), Lever's Port Sunlight (begun 1888) and Rowntree's New Earswick (begun 1902), though the emphasis on profitable housing investment and management, and sound if conventional housing design indicates that only rarely was company housing overtly philanthropic [Gaskell, 1986, *131*]. Some employers, like Baxters of Dundee, were dragged unwillingly into providing housing for workers, while geographical isolation still obliged others to do so, for example, steel and shipbuilding firms in Barrow [Roberts, 1978, *109*], railway companies at Crewe, Swindon and Wolverton in the 1840s, and collieries which commonly housed 3–11 per cent of their workforce in England and Wales, more in Durham and Scotland [Ball (Chapman) 1971, *294*; Daunton, 1980, *145*]. In some northern mill and mining towns company housing continued to be used to secure a regular labour force [Bedale, 1980, *50*; Marshall, 1968, *228*], and in Clydeside burghs from 1880 became part of a management strategy to obtain the compliance of supervisory grades, introduce new work practices, or dismiss inefficient workers on the pretext of delinquent rental payments [Melling, 1981, *258, 280*]. In this sense company housing extended capital-labour relations from the arena of production to that of consumption, and was well established as a means of influencing political allegiance in mill towns.

(c) The legislative framework and building control

There was no clearly defined housing policy *c.* 1850–80 and piecemeal legislation aimed to supplement rather than supplant the moral reform campaign. In a few cities – Leeds, Liverpool (1842), Manchester (1844/45), Nottingham, St Helens (1845),

Burnley, Newcastle (1846) – clauses in local Acts offered some control over new building, sewerage connections and cellar dwellings, as did the influential Metropolitan Building Act (1844) for London [Taylor, 1974, *46*; Beresford, 1971, *114*]. But adoption was not synonymous with enforcement and new buildings infrequently conformed to recommended light, air, space and sanitary standards [Gaskell, 1983, *5,30*]. As in the 1830s, it was cholera in 1848, a 'potent propogandist', and lax enforcement of the Public Health Act 1848 which concentrated efforts to frame national building regulations [Harper, 1985, *xix*]. The resulting model bye-laws were introduced by the Local Government Office Act in 1858 and adopted by 568 towns by 1868 [Gaskell, 1983, *21, 37*]. Though building regulations were for the first time generally available in the 1860s, their impact was modified by definitional problems, erratic local versions, court cases challenging municipal regulatory authority, and the continuing problem of enforcement, issues clarified only by a Royal Commission report in 1871. While the 1858 regulations were a breakthrough, the Public Health Act of 1875 presented intelligible consolidation since it was by this authority that the 1877 local government bye-laws required council supervision of street widths, building height, structural standards and drainage. (These powers had long been available through the Dean of Guild courts in some Scottish burghs, though for the majority they remained adoptive from 1862 and compulsory only from 1892. In Dublin byelaws were introduced, if loosely applied, from 1866 [Rodger, 1986, *185*; Daly, 1984, *282*].) Since by 1882 almost 1000 urban areas deployed building controls [Gaskell, 1983, *48*], the 1877 English regulations formalised geometric housing patterns already created by market forces in the principal cities and generalised them to all urban areas, but did so almost a century after the initial phase of rapid urbanisation.

However zealously enforced, building regulations in any one year affected only 1 per cent of the total housing stock. It took years to have much cumulative effect. So while bye-laws and moral reform adopted a long-term approach, immediate housing problems were confronted by four legislative initiatives: limitations on lodging houses, control of nuisances and overcrowding, sewer connections, and slum clearances [Wohl, 1977,

73]. The Common Lodging Houses Acts of 1851 and 1853, required such accommodation to be registered and inspected by police – controls extended in 1866 to all lodgings – but ambiguous drafting and their permissive nature meant the Acts were never used. Stemming from the view that overcrowding was a nuisance just as pernicious as sanitary defects, local authorities were empowered by the Nuisances Removal Act of 1855 to combat it by fines and court actions. Again the impact was slight, though, crucially, housing assumed both a place on the political agenda independently of public health and a change of gear, since defining overcrowding in terms of air space had implications for housing quantity. A third initiative, and a major landmark, was the obligation from 1866 to connect all houses to main sewers. Limitations on cellars used as accommodation were also contained in the Sanitary Act, 1866, but the significance of thirty-five public health and housing-related statutes in 1850–80 lay in the reorientation of central and local government relations, the challenge to presumed ultimate rights of property owners, creation of legislative precedents however ineffectual, and the engagement of a political will for long periods preoccupied with foreign policy [Lambert, 1963, *381*].

Slum clearance was the fourth legislative dimension. Municipalities' powers to purchase compulsorily and demolish limited insanitary areas reached the statute book in Torrens's Artizans' and Labourers' Dwellings Act, 1868 [Wohl, 1977, *84*]. Without the obligation to rehouse those made homeless, the Act offered little more than new nuisance removal powers, and had it been invoked would have exacerbated congestion in adjacent streets in precisely the manner achieved by railway companies in the station-building era of the 1840s [Kellett, 1969, *10*]. Rehousing responsibilities were, however, included in Cross's more comprehensive version, the Artizans' and Labourers' Dwellings Improvement Act, 1875, and though legal costs and high compensation to slum property owners limited its adoption to only twelve towns outside London, it fell ultimately to local authorities to rehouse if sales of cleared sites resulted in insufficient new housing [Yelling, 1986]. This 'creeping socialism' was not the first instance of local authority action for Liverpool (1864), Glasgow (1866), Edinburgh (1867) and Dundee (1871) had anticipated the Acts of 1868, 1875 and subsequent amending legislation in their own Local Improvement Acts designed to clear limited areas of insanitary housing, introduce new and wider streets and limit occupancy within houses [Allan, 1965, *604*; Butt (Chapman), 1971, *59*; Smith, 1980, *100*].

Taxes on building materials were abolished – bricks (1850), window tax (1851), glass (1860), timber (1866) – in an optimistic effort to improve the housing standard affordable by low-income groups. Cheap, fixed-interest loans – 4 per cent for 40 years – through the Public Works Loan Board from 1866, easier land transfer and, in Scotland, streamlined property title registration aimed to do the same. It seems unlikely that these benefits were enjoyed by tenants. Legislation to contain the environmental and personal damage caused by insanitary housing remained the sketchy framework for thirty years, and in no sense by linear progression, statutes attempted to reconcile the imperatives of urban renewal and minimum sanitary standards with the historic interests of private property.

7 A Late-Victorian and Edwardian Housing Crisis

No single factor generated a housing crisis at the end of the nineteenth century. Rather, it was the cumulative impact of interrupted supply, additional costs, higher rents and rates, and the flight of capital to more lucrative havens. The building boom of the 1870s added unprecedented numbers of new houses and temporarily offset some of the deficiencies of working-class housing. The trade cycle downturn of 1873 affected most towns and by 1876 the building boom had collapsed. Though there were temporary surges of building, for example, in 1880–1 and 1887–9, and some regional divergences – in London and Teesside boroughs – housebuilding for the low-paid, if not suspended between 1878 and 1892, was seriously curtailed (Figure 1) [Weber, 1955, *131*]. Gradual cyclical recovery in the 1890s with peaks in 1898 and 1903 again obscured the more fundamental problem of housing composition, that is insufficient numbers of affordable, convenient houses for the low-paid. Except where local economic prosperity sustained demand after 1905, residential building on the eve of the First World War was only one-third of peak production and even below levels of the depressed 1880s [Lewis, 1965, *App. 4*]. Builders' confidence, undermined by depression and innumerable bankruptcies in the 1880s, was threatened further by the limited, but ominous, market intervention of councils in property clearances, land sales and housebuilding [McKenna and Rodger, 1985, *212*]. Building regulations and declining labour productivity reinforced a deeper problem, the upward drift in real building costs, the combined effect of which increased rents and limited the extent to which housing problems could be solved through conventional reliance on the market.

Demolition by retailing and commercial interests had significantly reduced the availability of housing, but it was the railway companies, alone responsible for swallowing 5–9 per cent of the area of major cities [Kellett, 1969, *290*] and displacing up to 4 million residents between 1850 and 1900 [Waller, 1983, *161*], that had seriously intensified the housing problem. City-centre demolitions not only imposed onerous financial burdens on councils through excessive compulsory purchase payments [Yelling, 1987, *105*], but also exacerbated overcrowding in adjacent streets, inflated land prices, and caused real rent increases which between 1875 and 1900 amounted to 47 per cent, a rise unequalled in Victorian times [Weber, 1960/1, *64*]. Rates rose spectacularly too. In the same period, 1875–1900, rateable values increased 61 per cent and revenue from rates 141 per cent – in real terms by over 100 and 200 per cent respectively – with the burden falling disproportionately on the lower paid [Waller, 1983, *257*]. Property taxes squeezed landlords' returns, municipal intervention threatened ownership rights, and both adversely affected property values. Houseowners saw their assets decline 40–50 per cent between 1902 and 1912 following a 20 per cent reduction in working-class property values in the preceding decade [Offer, 1981, *268, 279*]. Consequently investors sought alternative outlets in consols, where yields increased 20 per cent between 1897 and 1907, and in record levels of foreign investment in the 1880s and 1900s [Cairncross, 1953, *45*]. Though builders' interest in low-income housing had always been confined to a few buoyant years at the peak of the local trade cycle, a new departure after 1900 was that investors and landlords, too, were uninterested in the finance and management of existing housing stocks. It is, then, from 1900 rather than from wartime rent restrictions (1915) or council housebuilding (1919) that the decline of the private landlord can be dated [Offer, 1981, *405*; Daunton, 1983, *295*].

With serious problems confronting new building and existing housing, and rents and rates increases absorbing significant portions of real wage increases, it was not surprising that from three different directions – political, intellectual and empirical – a powerful critique of *laissez-faire* developed in the 1880s, from which housing emerged fused to the broader issue of poverty. Politically, dissatisfaction with the achievements of the Cross and Torrens legislation enabled Salisbury and Chamberlain to project housing reform to the top of the party political agenda

53

by establishing the first Royal Commission on Working-Class Housing in 1883, chaired by Sir Charles Dilke, which reported in 1884–85 [Gauldie, 1974, *287*; Aalen (Bannon), 1985, *133*]. This secured prominent coverage officially and otherwise for housing issues and was sustained into the early twentieth century by issues such as rating reform, poverty relief and land value taxation. Intellectual critiques of late-Victorian capitalism emerged from historians, Oxford philosophers and influential individuals such as the Webbs and George Bernard Shaw and these critiques provided an ideological core for infant political movements such as the Social Democratic Federation, the Independent Labour Party and the Workmen's National Housing Council [Englander, 1983, *77*]. But the combination of a developing social theory based on ultimate state responsibility for welfare and of political manoeuvrings on social reform was given additional impetus by Andrew Mearns's *The Bitter Cry of Outcast London* (1883) and the *Pall Mall Gazette*'s widely read surveys of London poverty (1885). Though principally concerned with church non-attendance, Mearns's enquiries, like Mayhew's earlier revelations in the *Morning Chronicle* (1849–50), revealed poverty levels, immorality and wretched housing conditions, which both stung the public conscience and triggered public consciousness. They were also the stimulus for Charles Booth's (1889) and Seebohm Rowntree's (1901) empirical confirmation that approximately 30 per cent of London and York inhabitants lived below the poverty line, a conclusion which jolted Victorian confidence and added ammunition to those critical of income distribution after more than a century of industrialisation.

The 1891 Census provided for the first time statistical data on overcrowding. That market forces, bolstered by philanthropic efforts and suburbanisation, were overcoming housing deficiencies was an increasingly untenable view. Physical decrepitude was correlated with living conditions, as Medical Officers had long maintained, and if only generally acknowledged in the 1890s, was demonstrated by Boer War recruitment when, for example, a mere 18 per cent of 11,000 Manchester volunteers were physically acceptable for army duty. This slur on British military and imperial capabilities questioned 'national efficiency' and endorsed the view that a faltering late-Victorian economic performance was partially attributable to the quality of labour.

In this climate of opinion housing was no longer considered as an adjunct to sanitary policy. Pragmatic approaches typified by the Cross and Torrens legislation were superseded by a more expansive intent – council housing, town planning and cheap suburban transport – though the underlying motive for such concessions was, in the eyes of new Liberals such as Hobhouse and Nettlefold, to improve the quality of housing affordable by the working class and thus preserve rather than jeopardise the structure of property relations [Castells, 1977]. Even so, the new initiatives eroded capitalist interests: private builders ceded a segment of the building industry to municipalities, land utilisation and disposition was subject to external controls, and new transport routes produced centrifugal intrusions into comfortable suburbia. Just as the 1919 electoral pledge 'Homes for heroes' was intended to secure social stability and the compliance of labour [Swenarton, 1981, *78*], so in the 1890s against the backdrop of an extended franchise, 'New Unionism' and a wave of strikes the same objectives implicitly applied as concessions were sought and obtained from property interests.

(i) MARKET INTERVENTION: COMPLEMENTARY
     APPROACHES TO HOUSING PROBLEMS

Within defined limits market intervention was increasingly acceptable to emergent neo-classical economics, and so given the magnitude and intransigence of Victorian housing problems, municipal building and town and country planning were seen as correctives to, not as replacements for, the prevailing ideology. Indeed the Royal Commission reports, 1884–5, still envisaged private enterprise as central to future housebuilding and the permissive rather than imperative tone of its legislative outcome, the Housing of the Working Classes Act, 1890, conveyed its defence of *status quo* interests. However, Part III of the 1890 Act allowed councils to initiate new housing projects rather than simply replacements on cleared sites, and if there had been precedents in Liverpool (St Martin's cottages 1869), London and Edinburgh, this extension of general housebuilding functions was more actively grasped by

55

municipalities [Steffel, 1976, *163*; Gaskell, 1976, *195*; Hopkins, 1978, *247*]. Between 1890 and 1904, eighty councils borrowed twice as much from the Public Works Loan Board as had been sought for housing improvements in the fifteen years preceding the Act, with Dublin, London and Liverpool councils most vigorous [Daly, 1984, *318*; Gauldie, 1974, *294*]. Even so, of the national housing stock rented below £20 p.a., that is, affordable by the working class, only 0.25 per cent was municipally owned in 1912, and like model dwelling associations, corporations discriminated between tenants on the basis of the regularity of incomes [Pooley, 1985, *79*].

Nor had town planning achieved much by 1914 [Ashworth, 1954, *190*; Sutcliffe, 1981, *86*]. Utopian ideals for comprehensive planning advanced municipal intervention beyond the narrow technical requirements of clearances and found expression in a new town (Letchworth 1903), garden suburbs (Oldham 1906, Hampstead 1907, Bristol 1909), fourteen co-partnership housing schemes, and a handful of employers' communities (Bournville, Port Sunlight, New Earswick) [Swenarton, 1981, *5*; Gaskell, 1981, *34*]. The comprehensive intent was also present in legislative form, the Town Planning Act, 1909 [Cherry, 1974, *34, 64*], but this regulated only suburban development and, more seriously, failed to provide local authorities with powers compulsorily to purchase land beyond their boundaries. Town planning initiatives before 1914, therefore, did little more than establish professional credentials, indicate new though limited directions, and encourage low-density suburban estates likely to have developed anyway; they barely addressed the underlying problems of working-class housing.

Commuting as a means of encouraging working-class suburban migration to relieve central housing congestion was similar in intent to town planning initiatives and adopted with greater conviction in the 1880s. Workmen's fares, introduced as early as 1844, were too high, services were infrequent and unsynchronised with working hours, and stations were inconveniently located [Dyos, 1953, *18*]. London railway companies, motivated by revenue considerations, rectified certain of these problems from the mid 1860s and this formed a preparatory stage before the Cheap Trains Act, 1883, repealed a passenger tax on workmen's tickets and compelled companies to introduce cheap fares. In most towns the 1883 legislation had little effect on housing problems because for the poor, credit networks, shopping patterns and earning opportunities for family members were dislocated in a suburban setting. Fares remained a disproportionate element of weekly wages and were insufficiently offset by lower rents. The limited extent of working-class commuting in the 1890s was reflected in the modest daily sales of workmen's tickets in Liverpool and Birmingham which like most cities before the motor age remained easily crossed on foot [Kellett, 1969, *93*]. The exception was London. Pressure from London County Council and the Board of Trade after 1890 led to fare reductions and service improvements. In 1883, 106 workmen's trains covered 735 miles each day; by 1914, 2000 trains covered 14,000 miles and carried ½ million workmen daily from the suburbs. In a 6–8 mile radius from central London workmen's tickets represented 40 per cent of all ticket sales.

In London and in provincial cities alike, the real beneficiaries of cheap railway fares after 1883, as with trams from the 1870s, were not those in most urgent need of rehousing but artisans and lower and middle-class shop and office workers. For them the cumulative effect of rising real incomes in the last quarter of the nineteenth century was most tangibly expressed by moving to new and distinctive suburbs and commuting to an increasingly well-defined central business district. Cheap fares did not create the suburbs; they were created for the new suburbans. Real income improvements permitted artisans and the petit bourgeoisie participation in a suburban option previously available only to the middle class, with consequential tensions as different social strata intruded at the margins of, and even leapfrogged, formerly exclusive middle-class dormitories. Commuting and the formation of distinct artisan suburbs at the end of the nineteenth century contributed to further residential segregation, leaving an undifferentiated corps of low-paid slum dwellers in the centre trapped by irregular earnings, high rents and immobility.

(ii) PROPERTY POLITICS: TENSION AND CRISIS 1880–1914

That late-Victorian property interests were not progressing towards an equilibrium was reflected in mounting tension at three levels: municipal, national and individual property relations.

(a) Ratepayers and municipal financial pressures

Before the 1870s, ratepayers through their elected representatives periodically had been able to restrain local expenditure programmes [Hennock, 1963, *217*; McCord, 1978, *22*]. In the late nineteenth century statutory council responsibilities – gas, water, parks, medical and sanitary inspections, education and loan charges on related capital projects – raised local expenditures uncontrollably: by 187 per cent between 1875 and 1900, and over the longer span, 1870–1910, by 316 per cent [Feinstein, 1972, *T132*][15]. To finance this local taxation was levied principally on property, which felt the burden acutely either when general prices were falling, as from the 1880s, or when property values declined, as from the 1890s. Rates were calculated according to the gross annual value of land and buildings, that is on fixed property; income, dividends and profits were exempt [Daunton, 1983, *220*]. In theory local taxes fell on occupiers, but in practice owners increasingly shouldered the burden. As articulated by shopkeepers, small businessmen, and property owners, ratepayers criticised local tax assessments on three grounds: (a) regressiveness, since the poor paid disproportionately, as did retailers and workshops, (b) equity, as no account of users' circumstances was taken to determine rateable value, and (c) exemptions on unoccupied buildings or vacant land, which together with 'betterment' (i.e. windfall gains from urban land appreciation) encouraged owners to delay property development.

Inequitable local taxation was not new. But the impact was more intensely felt and bitterly resented by ratepayers after 1880 since a narrow and regressive tax base meant that rising municipal expenditure could only be met by increasing tax rates. So though the tax base 1875–1900 expanded by 61 per cent, revenue raised from rates increased 141 per cent and the average national rate in the £ rose from 3s. 6d. in 1885, to 4s. 2d. in 1895, 6s. in 1905 and 6s. 9d. in 1914 [Waller, 1983, *257*]. Revenue-producing council activities and, after 1888, revised central government contributions in the form of block grants offered limited financial relief to local authorities who turned to a reduction of allowances to property owners for collecting tenant's rates as an economy measure [Daunton, 1983, *203*]. In so doing councils further undermined the profitability of house ownership and management. Rates increases were reflected in rent increases and working-class occupiers became enmeshed in the conflict between local authority and landlords' interests. Tenant radicalism resulted. Possibly of greater long-term significance, this conflict over the administration and division of rates drove a wedge between middle-class owner occupiers, who favoured direct payment of rates, and small property owners, who advocated allowances for undertaking the collection of taxes [Englander, 1983, *54*]. Internally ruptured, ratepayers' factions on city councils lost their former leverage; nationally they never developed an identity. Property interests, therefore, were a late- nineteenth-century sacrifice on the financial altar of civic expansionism.

(b) Property interests and national politics

The severe impact of late-Victorian rates burdens was an object of deep concern to both Liberal and Conservative parties and the justice of relief measures was widely accepted. Fundamental disagreement existed, however, over how to implement rating reform [Offer, 1981, *163*]. The Conservatives' solution endorsed the existing system but sought to alter the balance in two ways: (a) by levying less from houses and land (regarded as having a common interest) and more from other assets and sources of income, and (b) by accepting central financial responsibility for additional local administrative functions. Liberals, conversely, claimed not that houses and land paid too little tax but that the shift between them adversely affected housing interests which paid too much compared to land. When, in the wake of revised local authority administration, Conservatives in 1888 extended rate support grants to rural and church interests fundamental tax reform on property was jettisoned. As a means of annexing

59

further electoral support the Conservatives sought to encourage owner occupation and consequently landlords' interests became a political liability and thus expendable [Offer, 1981, *209*; Englander, 1983, *80*]. This created an opportunity for radical Liberals to propose a tax on land along the lines popularised by Henry George in *Poverty and Progress* (1881). Land values appreciated because of population pressure and municipal improvements, that is, independently of landowners' actions. This 'unearned increment' in value encouraged land hoarding, diminished supplies of land for housing, raised rents both initially and as leases matured, and contributed to slums and overcrowding [Reeder, 1961, *418*]. Widely supported by members of the Association of Municipal Corporations in the 1890s, land value taxation was embraced by Liberals as an integrated housing reform and income redistribution measure – a 'single tax', though private bills introduced in each year 1899–1905 made no progress [Waller, 1983, *261*; Pointing and Bulos, 1984, *469*]. Land value taxation proposals encountered three difficulties: (a) site value increases were less than formerly, (b) a land value tax might be passed to occupiers, so worsening housing conditions, and (c) small property owners opposed land taxation since as freeholders they, too, benefited from rising site values, as did builders, who used appreciating ground rents to raise working capital (see p. 25). Despite Conservative government opposition to land taxation and endorsement of the existing system of Treasury grants to local authorities by the Royal Commission on Local Taxation reports in 1901,[16] the 'housing famine' as sustained by the local taxation issue remained a live political topic until the First World War. Lloyd George incorporated taxes on undeveloped land in the 'Peoples' Budget', 1909, and the issues were resurrected in the 1914 Budget which also proposed the abolition of rates [Gilbert, 1978, *132*; Murray, 1973, *558*]. Ultimately, it was the scale and interconnectedness of the housing problem and the land question which derailed the administrative reforms and redistributive intent of early-twentieth-century Liberals. Simultaneously the unresolved difficulties of local taxation consigned property interests to decline.

(c) Individual conflicts: landlords versus tenants

The predicament of municipal finance and its national political dimension pressurised landlords to search for more efficient property management strategies which inevitably had an impact on tenants' interests. This was not new since throughout the nineteenth century property owners' associations and those of tenants sought to gain a marginal advantage [Bedale, 1980, *61*]. For example, the Small Tenements Recovery Act, 1838, dispensed with the landlord's need for a court order to repossess a house, yet tenants could neutralise these sweeping powers by vandalising or selling fixtures, and by 'shooting the moon' (flitting) [Englander, 1983, *20*; Daly, 1984, *286*]. Such hostility was not uncommon in nineteenth-century landlord-tenant relations and was even carried into the arena of Edwardian municipal housing since 42 per cent of tenants leaving Liverpool council houses in 1903–9 were evicted by the Corporation [Pooley, 1985, *83*]. Nowehere was this landlord-tenant friction greater than in late-Victorian Scotland. Evictions rose appreciably from 1880, escalating in Glasgow from about 3200 p.a. in the 1870s to over 20,000 by 1906, and landlords' common law actions to obtain rents from the proceeds of forced sales of tenants' personal possessions more than doubled during 1899–1910, though they declined thereafter [Englander, 1983, *42*]. In urban Scotland house factors dominated rent collection; in Glasgow (1908) 80 per cent compared to 16 per cent in Birmingham (1898) of property was managed by middlemen who assured owners of an agreed rental income while themselves accepting responsibility for collection, and sometimes for repairs and insurance too [Morgan and Daunton, 1983, *274*]. In Scottish burghs cartel-like rent fixing existed amongst house factors but it was prompt eviction and sequestration for rent arrears which were their standard procedures, and like bailiffs, as the agents of proprietors they were reviled by tenants for their insensitive preoccupation with rent collection [Damer, 1980, *91*]. Tension surfaced over the 'missive', an undertaking by Scottish tenants to lease for a year. Shorter lets were advocated by tenants and necessitated by municipal finances to limit rates arrears; to sweeten their introduction landlords were given even stronger powers of summary eviction in 1911, though still

61

obliged for a small commission to collect occupiers' rates [Daunton, 1983, *211*].

Had demand for and supply of housing remained in equilibrium rents would have remained static. They did not. Fundamental disequilibrium as indicated by the 20 per cent upward drift of normally 'sticky' rents during 1875–1900 [Weber, 1960/6, *64*] – more than the increase in money wages[17] – reflected a mounting housing crisis. When somewhat unreasonably, since qualitative improvements in accommodation were also involved, tenants blamed landlords, latent hostility developed into outright conflict. This took several forms, including a political presence in the Workmens' National Housing Council, formed in 1898. But rent strikes in English boroughs in 1911–13, anticipating those on Clydeside in 1915, signalled the widespread and mounting frustration of tenants and their perceptions of endemic housing problems [Melling, 1983, *19*; Englander, 1983, *181*].

8 Comfort and Housing Amenity

If, from the supply viewpoint of building and property management, adverse trends presented critical problems, strengthening demand to some extent mitigated the pressure on housing quality in late-Victorian Britain. Precisely the same crucial factor that underlay the renewed suburban impulse – increased incomes – was responsible for this late-Victorian consumer boom. Between 1860 and 1895 per capita real incomes rose 107 per cent, slackening from 1895 to 1913 to just 7 per cent [Feinstein, 1972, *T8, T14*], equivalent to + 2.1 per cent p.a. 1860–95, and + 0.5 per cent p.a. 1895–1913.[18] Though real wages advanced less (+ 1.5 per cent p.a.) they enabled those regularly employed to participate in improved standards of domestic comfort. Sales of pianos, linoleum, curtains, wallpaper, cabinets and a deluge of *bric-à-brac* were demonstrations of this increased purchasing power [Fraser, 1981, *193*]. Structurally, a back extension to terraced houses (see Figure 3) provided a separate scullery, isolating cooking and washing, and thus women, from a family living room, and wider house frontages allowed a porch, hallway and self-contained parlour to further differentiate room functions within the house [Muthesius, 1982, *99*]. Stained glass, plaster and other decorative details were expressions of affordable domestic improvements also externally represented by bay windows, stuccoed brickwork and ornate facades. But it was the widespread availability of piped water and gas after 1890 which materially altered domestic routines. The completion of many municipal reservoirs and sewers from the 1870s provided constant water supplies and enabled a sanitary 'revolution' – the substitution of water-borne sewage disposal for the laborious emptying of decomposing, semi-solid waste from middens, ash- or pail-closets – to take place from the 1890s [Daunton, 1983, *256*]. High-rise Scottish tenements made the introduction of water and WCs difficult and expensive so that in 1914 the overwhelming majority of the Scottish working class still shared WCs, washing facilities and even sinks, though here, too, there was an unmistakable improvement after 1890 [Rodger, 1986, *162*].

Though the coal-burning range dominated the provision of economical heat, hot water and cooking facilities until 1914 [Ravetz, 1968, *456*], the flexibility and convenience of gas was increasingly appreciated by working-class users following the invention of slot meters and incandescent mantles in the late 1880s [Burnett, 1978, *21*]. These overcame the inconvenience of infrequent bills, uncomfortable summer heat from the kitchen range and unpredictable paraffin or sooty gas lighting in winter. Though still more expensive than coal, the differential narrowed from the 1880s so that gas prices did not present an insuperable barrier to consumers of all classes wishing to translate rising incomes into improved comfort and amenity [Daunton, 1983, *245*]. In most towns by 1914 between 30–60 per cent of consumers had gas cookers. The domestic impact of technological change on cooking and washing was considerable, but it also complemented a Victorian image of a cosy, comfortable home as the cornerstone of moral order.

Within the house both comfort and amenity were improved from the 1870s since space and other facilities were shared among fewer family members. For marriages registered during 1881–6 compared to those in the 1850s, completed family size fell by 33 per cent for the middle classes and by 21 per cent for skilled, 20 per cent for semi-skilled, 15 per cent for unskilled and rural labourers, and 10 per cent for miners.[19] The transition to a smaller family size took place in each decade from the 1870s so that by 1910 the number of births per family (3.0) was almost half that of the 1870s (5.8). The phenomenon affected every occupational group but occurred earlier and was initially more pronounced amongst the middle class. This differential fall in fertility according to occupation reinforced existing mechanisms for residential segregation. Though doubts exist as to whether the working class copied middle-class family limitation – the synchronised timing suggests an independent decision – a common influence was the competing lure of consumer products at a time of rising child-rearing costs. Education and factory

64

legislation restricted potential contributions to household income from working children in the last quarter of the nineteenth century, while for the middle class the rising costs of gentility, principally the wages of dependable domestic servants, coincided with increased fees for school and profess-ional training. Across the broad spectrum of incomes large families became an increasing, yet increasingly avoidable, financial burden and from the 1870s reactions to this resulted in smaller families and a decisive shift in consumer preferences towards greater comfort, amenity and domestic space.

9 Conclusion

Hostile living conditions have been seen as a logical, if unfortunate, by-product of industrialisation. Slums, thus interpreted, were a casualty of economic progress, the product of unrestrained market forces in a vacuum of building control. Alternatively, low wages and slums can be viewed as a precondition for the dynamic process of economic growth. Minimum wages, and thus low housing quality, were an integral part of nineteenth-century British competitiveness which assisted export performance, overseas investment and ultimately balance of payments strength. Nineteenth-century housing, thus viewed, was part of a systematic process which reproduced labour for the purposes and continuation of industrial capitalism. To have actively redistributed resources by means of higher wages, investment in social overhead capital or restraints on rents would have been inconsistent with the prevailing economic philosophy underpinning Victorian prosperity.

While private gains to land and capital outweighed social costs there was little reason to address the slum problem, and in fact suburbanisation temporarily sidestepped the environmental consequences and postponed intervention without disturbing either the mechanism of low wages or the structure and distribution of wealth and power. But, pricked by Christian consciences, panicked by the fear of disease, and punctured by developing public transport, the insularity of suburbia could not indefinitely neglect deficient housing standards. How best to contain the contamination was approached with considerable reluctance. Successively the sequence of sanitary provisions, permissive legislation and bye-law regulation, 'model dwellings', municipal clearances and site redevelopment, and taxation proposals each sought to limit the concessions required from property interests and were geared to re-establishing working-class independence. Even council housing, town planning and inexpensive suburban transport, by ostensibly extending choice to those in housing need, sought to restore individual liberty and self-reliance. And despite these interventionist overtones housing subsidies were rejected and faith in market forces reaffirmed.

This reluctant reformism was in fact overtaken in the last quarter of the nineteenth century by wider social and economic forces associated with rising real wages and reduced family sizes, and it was these influences more than the combined impact of housing reform efforts which contributed to the upward drift in standards of accommodation and comfort for a majority of the population. More fundamentally, perceptions of housing had altered with the realisation that it had a considerable impact on both the quality and quiescence of labour, as well as on military capabilities and national economic efficiency. Nowhere was this better captured than on the dustjacket of Reiss's book, *The Home I Want*, published in 1919, where a demobilised solider declared: 'You cannot get an A1 population out of C3 homes.'

Notes and References

1 Report of the Select Committee on the Health of Towns, *PP 1840 XI*, vi, viii, ix; *The Times*, 4 Dec. 1844, 6e.

2 D. E. Baines, *Migration in a Mature Economy: Emigration and Internal Migration in England and Wales, 1861–1900* (1985), p. 219.

3 L. Soltow, 'Long run changes in British income inequality', *Economic History Review*, 21 (1968), 17–29.

4 M. W. Flinn, 'Trends in real wages 1750–1850', *Economic History Review*, 27 (1974), 408.

5 N. F. R. Crafts, *British Economic Growth During the Industrial Revolution* (1985), pp. 98, 112.

6 P. H. Lindert and J. G. Williamson, 'English workers' living standards during the industrial revolution', *Economic History Review*, 36 (1983), Tables 3–5.

7 E. A. Wrigley and R. S. Schofield, *The Population History of England 1541–1871* (1981), p. 529.

8 B. R. Mitchell and P. Deane, *Abstract of British Historical Statistics* (1962), pp. 343–5; B. E. Supple, 'Income and demand 1860–1914', in R. Floud and D. McCloskey (eds), *The Economic History of Britain since 1700*, vol. 2, *1860 – the 1970s* (1981), pp. 121–43.

9 1st Annual Report of the Registrar General, *PP 1839 VI*, App.Q.79.

10 E. Jones, *A Social Geography of Belfast* (1960), p. 51; Census of Ireland, 1851, *PP 1856 XXXI* [2134], Pt.VI, 410.

11 Census of England and Wales 1911, *PP 1912–13 CXI*, Vol. II, Tables XLVI, XLVII, and Census of Scotland 1911, *PP 1913 C*, Tables VI, XL, XLVIII.

12 A. Saunders, *Regent's Park* (1969), p. 86.

13 D. Fraser, *Urban Politics in Victorian England. The Structure of Politics in Victorian Cities* (1976).

14 Royal Commission on Factories, *PP 1833 XX*.

15 Mitchell and Deane, *Abstract*, p. 418.
16 Royal Commission on Local Taxation, *PP 1901 XXIV*, 413.
17 Mitchell and Deane, *Abstract*, p. 344.
18 Supple, 'Income and demand', 123.
19 D. E. Baines, 'The labour supply and the labour market 1860–1914' in Floud and McCloskey, *Economic History*, p. 147.

Bibliography

An extensive literature exists on housing and urban development. Excellent bibilographical surveys of housing and related topics are published annually in a classified list in the *Urban History Yearbook*. Select bibliographies are also available in the works by Offer, Dennis, Sutcliffe (1972) and Englander. Individual town histories are not cited here, neither are transport, town planning, local government or public health except where these have a direct impact on housing, but annotated references are provided in G. H. Martin and S. McIntyre, *A Bibliography of British and Irish Municipal History* (1972) and H. J. Dyos's 'Agenda for Urban Historians' in *The Study of Urban History* (1968). Contemporary works provide valuable insights, e.g. O. Hill, *Homes of the London Poor* (1875) and A. Mearns, *The Bitter Cry of Outcast London* (1883) (Cass reprints, 1970); A. F. Weber, *The Growth of Cities in the Nineteenth Century* (1899; Cornell reprint 1963). Lynn Lees and Andrew Lees *The Rise of Urban Britain* (New York, 1984) reprints 35 titles. Unless otherwise indicated, the place of publication in the select list below is London.

Allan, C. M., 'The genesis of British urban development with special reference to Glasgow', *Economic History Review*, 17 (1965), 598–613. Careful analysis of City Improvement Trust slum clearances. Should be read with Smith on Edinburgh.

Alonso, W., 'A theory of the urban land market', *Papers and Proceedings of the Regional Science Association*, 6 (1960), 149–58. Provides a spatial model of users' differential access requirements to city centre which determines rental levels and thus land usage. (See also Whitehand).

Ashworth, W., *The Genesis of British Town Planning* (1954) Pathbreaking work viewing municipal intervention as a progressive trend towards comprehensive planning.

Aspinall, P.J., 'The internal structure of the housebuilding industry in nineteenth-century cities', in J.H. Johnson and C.G. Pooley (eds), *The Structure of Nineteenth Century Cities* (1982), pp. 75–105. Examines Cooney's 'master builders' thesis in relation to Sheffield.

Bannon, M.J. (ed.), *The Emergence of Irish Planning 1880–1920* (Dublin, 1985), pp. 131–88. Valuable chapters by Daly and Aalen on working-class housing in Dublin.

Beattie, S., *A Revolution in London Housing: LCC Housing Architects and their Work 1893–1914* (1980). Illustrated (r)evolution of municipal housing with interesting insights into early administrative apparatus.

Bedale, C., 'Property relations and housing policy: Oldham in the late nineteenth and early twentieth centuries', in J. Melling (ed.) (1980), pp. 37–72. Shows company housing concerned with labour supplies and wage costs, and landlords with maximising rentier incomes; both caused landlord-tenant friction.

Beresford, M.W., 'The back-to-back house in Leeds 1787–1937', in S.D. Chapman (ed.) (1971), pp. 93–132. Convincing explanation of the emergence of back-to-back housing.

Bowley, M., *Innovations in Building Materials* (1960). Part II still provides a major survey of technical change in nineteenth-century building industry. See also Cooney and Powell.

Burnett, J., *A Social History of Housing 1815–1970* (Newton Abbot, 1978). Offers the best and most accessible descriptive introduction.

Caffyn, L., *Workers' Housing in West Yorkshire 1750–1920* (1986). Illustrated evolution of variations in vernacular architecture.

Cairncross, A.K., *Home and Foreign Investment 1870–1913* (Cambridge, 1953). Presents a general 'model' of alternating factor flows, and analyses the dynamics of the Glasgow building industry.

Cannadine, D.N., *Lords and Landlords: the Aristocracy and the Towns 1774–1967* (Leicester, 1980). Estate development strategies in Birmingham and Eastbourne combined with masterly command of sources on landownership generally.

Carter, H. and Wheatley, S., *Merthyr Tydfil in 1851: A Study of the Spatial Structure of a Welsh Industrial Town* (Cardiff, 1982). Extensive mapping of town though the statistical analysis of social areas lacks a human dimension.

Castells, M., *The Urban Question* (1977). Based on contemporary French urban experience but challenges the thesis that there was a distinct cultural experience associated with cities. Urban environment treated as a point of consumption with housing a crucial element in the maintenance of production and social relations.

Chalklin, C. W., *The Provincial Towns of Georgian England: A Study of the Building Process 1740–1820* (1974). Virtually the sole serious study of housing and building in the formative period.

Chapman, S. D. (ed.), *The History of Working-Class Housing: A Symposium* (1971). Influential, detailed studies by Wohl (London), Butt (Glasgow), Beresford (Leeds), Chapman (Nottingham), Treble (Liverpool), Chapman and Bartlett (Birmingham), Smith (mainly Rochdale, Milnrow, Middleton), Ball, (Ebbw Vale).

Checkland, O and S., 'Housing policy: the formative years', *Town Planning Review*, 46 (1975), 315–22. Review of Gauldie (1974) and Tarn (1973). Integrates limited philanthropic housing achievements into the prevailing market ideology.

Cherry, G. E., *The Evolution of British Town Planning* (1974). Chapter 1 provides a useful summary, but Ashworth (1954), Sutcliffe (1981) more comprehensive.

Cleary, E. J., *The Building Society Movement* (1965). Heavy going but the only detailed treatment.

Conzen, M. R. G., 'The morphology of towns in Britain during the industrial era', in J. W. R. Whitehand (ed.), *The Urban Landscape: Historical Development and Management: Papers by M. R. G. Conzen* (1981), pp. 87–126. Contributions to spatial interpretation of towns of considerable influence on historical geographers.

Cooney, E. W., 'Capital exports and investment in building in Britain and the USA, 1856–1914', *Economica*, 16 (1949), 347–54. Anticipates Cairncross's and Thomas's 'Atlantic Economy' thesis.

Cooney, E. W., 'The origins of the Victorian master builders', *Economic History Review*, 8 (1955), 167–76. Identifies four types of building firm.

Cooney, E. W., 'The building industry', in R. Church (ed.), *The Dynamics of Victorian Business: Problems and Perspectives to the*

1870s (1980), pp. 142–60. Informative summary of organisation and technology but now needs to be supplemented with Price (1980).

Corfield, P. J., *The Impact of English Towns* (1982). With Chalklin forms an essential background to Victorian housing.

Cowlard, K. A., 'The identification of social (class) areas and their place in nineteenth century urban development', *Transactions Institute of British Geographers*, 4 (1979), 239–57. Concludes that there were well established one-class areas in mid-century Wakefield.

Crossick, G. J., 'Urban society and the petty bourgeoisie in nineteenth century Britain' in D. Fraser and A. Sutcliffe (eds) (1983), pp. 307–26. Interesting comments on sources of savings for housebuilding.

Daly, M. E., *Dublin – The Deposed Capital: A Social and Economic History 1860–1914* (Cork, 1984). Useful Irish perspective on suburbs and working-class housing with strong English parallels.

Damer, S., 'State, class and housing: Glasgow 1885–1919' in J. Melling (ed.) (1980), pp. 73–112. Sets housing in the context of labour unrest and class tensions, and integrates these and the Royal Commission reports of 1884–5 with the contradictions of late-Victorian capitalism and imperialism.

Daunton, M. J., *Coal Metropolis: Cardiff 1870–1914* (Leicester, 1977). Study of building and urban development significant far beyond Cardiff.

Daunton, M. J., 'Miners' houses: South Wales and the Great Northern Coalfield', *International Review of Social History*, 25, (1980), 143–75. Variable regional reliance on company housing explained by different managerial strategies.

Daunton, M. J., *House and Home in the Victorian City: Working Class Housing 1850–1914* (1983). Essential reading. Valuable contributions on landlordism and amenities within the house. With Offer and Englander represents the most important recent contributions to the literature.

Davidoff, L., 'Mastered for life: servant and wife in Victorian and Edwardian England', *Journal of Social History*, 7 (1974), 406–28. Powerful examination of gender divisions and the home (see also Summers).

Davidoff, L. and Hall, C., *Family Fortunes: Men and Women of the*

73

English Middle Class 1780–1850 (1987). Excellent analytical chapters on 'domestic ideology' and 'middle-class homes'.

Dennis, R. J., *English Industrial Cities of the Nineteenth Century: a Social Geography* (Cambridge, 1984). Immensely helpful synthesis of various geographical and spatial theories of housing from a historical geographer concerned to explain rather than merely to map.

Doe, V. S., 'Some developments in middle class housing in Sheffield 1830–1875' in S. Pollard and C. Holmes (eds), *Essays in the Economic and Social History of South Yorkshire* (Sheffield, 1976), pp. 174–85. Useful addition, with more depth than Tarn (Simpson and Lloyd), to sparse literature on middle-class housing.

Dyos, H. J., 'Workmen's fares in south London 1860–1914', *Journal of Transport History*, 1 (1953), 3–19. (With other Dyos work on urban transport reprinted in D. Cannadine and D. Reeder (eds), *Exploring the Urban Past: Essays in Urban History by H. J. Dyos* (Cambridge, 1982).

Dyos, H. J., *Victorian Suburb: a Study of the Growth of Camberwell* (Leicester, 1961). Seminal work on housing, building and estate development. (See also Dyos, 1968).

Dyos, H. J., 'The slums of Victorian London', *Victorian Studies*, 11 (1967), 5–40. Investigates the term 'slum', its origins and nature.

Dyos, H. J., 'The speculative builders and developers of Victorian London', *Victorian Studies*, 11 (1968), 641–90.

Dyos, H. J. and Reeder, D. A., 'Slums and suburbs' in H. J. Dyos and M. Wolff (eds), *The Victorian City: Images and Reality* (1973) pp. 359–86. Elegant argument that slums underpinned Victorian prosperity and suburbs emphasised the process.

Elliott, B. and McCrone, D., 'Urban development in Edinburgh: a contribution to the political economy of place', *Scottish Journal of Sociology*, 4 (1980), 1–26. Informative small area study of investors, landlords and landowners.

Engels, F., *The Housing Question* (1870; Moscow edn 1979). Amid the jargon of a polemic against Proudhon, illuminating contemporary view of 'How the bourgeoisie solves the housing question'.

Englander, D., *Landlord and Tenant in Urban Britain 1838–1918*

(Oxford, 1983). Changing legal basis of landlords' and tenants' rights explored as a background to politicisation of housing interests.

Feinstein, C. H. (a) 'Capital formation in Great Britain' in P. Mathias and M. M. Postan (eds), *The Cambridge Economic History of Europe*, vol. 7, part 1 (1978), pp. 28–96. Tentative estimates of housebuilding investment but the best available. (b) For firmer estimates of the later period see Feinstein, *National Income, Expenditure and Output of the United Kingdom, 1855–1965* (Cambridge, 1972), T88–9.

Forster, C. A., *Court Housing in Kingston upon Hull* (Hull, 1972). University of Hull Occasional Papers in Geography, no. 19. Informative and neglected study of local housing variants.

Foster, J., 'How imperial London preserved its slums', *International Journal of Urban and Regional Research*, 3 (1979), 93–114. Criticises Wohl (1977) for neglecting the context of capitalist production relations and state power in explaining housing conditions.

Fraser, D. and Sutcliffe, A. (eds), *The Pursuit of Urban History* (1983). Book 3 deals with nineteenth-century housing, with an excellent survey by Sutcliffe 'In pursuit of the urban variable'.

Fraser, W. H., *The Coming of the Mass Market 1850–1914* (1981). Chapters on shelter and furnishing should be supplemented with Daunton (1983) and Rubinstein.

Gaskell, S. M., 'Sheffield City Council and the development of suburban areas prior to World War I' in S. Pollard and C. Holmes (eds), *Essays in the Economic and Social History of South Yorkshire* (Sheffield, 1976), pp. 187–202. Presses a claim for Sheffield as a vigorous council housebuilder.

Gaskell, S. M., ' "The suburb salubrious": town planning in practice' in A. Sutcliffe (ed.), *British Town Planning: the Formative Years* (Leicester, 1981), pp. 16–61. Wide-ranging study of the garden city movement.

Gaskell, S. M., *Building Control: National Legislation and the Introduction of Local Bye-Laws in Victorian England* (1983). Useful account of chronological development of building regulations considered in a broader and more analytical setting than Harper (1985).

Gaskell, S. M., *Model Housing: from the Great Exhibition to the*

Festival of Britain (1986). Identifies chronological shifts in 'models' of working-class housing.

Gauldie, E., *Cruel Habitations: A History of Working Class Housing* (1974). Sound on philanthropy and early legislation, though rather compartmentalised presentation lacks analytical rigour and takes a Whiggish or progressive view of housing.

Gilbert, B. B., 'David Lloyd George, the reform of British landholding and the budget of 1914', *Historical Journal*, 21 (1978), 117–41. Evaluates Lloyd George's land and property taxation proposals as part of an attempt to reform British urban (and rural) land tenure, housing and wage systems.

Gordon, G., 'The status areas of early to mid-Victorian Edinburgh', *Transactions Institute of British Geographers*, 4 (1979), 168–91. Identifies and maps residential patterns according to rateable values.

Habakkuk, H. J., 'Fluctuations in housebuilding in Britain and the United States in the nineteenth century', *Journal of Economic History*, 22 (1962), 198–230. Penetrating critique of 'Atlantic Economy' thesis: shifts emphasis to closer alignment of building and domestic trade cycles.

Harper, R. H., *Victorian Building Regulations: Summary Tables of the Principal English Building Acts and Model By-Laws 1840–1914* (1985), xi–xxix. Provides crisp summary of legislative milestones but Gaskell (1983) presents a better background and analysis.

Harvey, D., *Social Justice and the City* (1973). Reviews social processes and urban spatial form and concludes that the internal dynamics of industrial capitalism – appropriation, exploitation and the circulation of surplus value – produced a growing concentration of fixed investment, i.e. housing.

Hennock, E. P., 'Finance and politics in urban local government in England, 1835–1900', *Historical Journal*, 6 (1963), 212–25. Ratepayers' periodic influence on councils convincingly explained as reactions to surges in municipal expenditure. Influence in decline *c*. 1890.

Hobhouse, H., *Thomas Cubitt: Master Builder* (1971). Unsurpassed business history with considerable detail and technical detail on the building industry.

Hopkins, E., 'Working class housing in the smaller industrial town in the nineteenth century: Stourbridge – a case study',

Midland History, 3–4 (1978), 230–54. Presents unusual data on housing space according to floor areas.

Jackson, J., 'Housing areas in mid-Victorian Wigan and St Helens', *Transactions Institute of British Geographers*, 6 (1981), 413–32. Argues that declining mid-century local economic fortunes led to atypical stagnation in housing standards.

Jones, G. S., *Outcast London: a Study in the Relationship Between Classes in Victorian Society* (1971). Casual London labour market powerfully analysed as a background to urban degeneration and housing crisis after 1880.

Kellett, J. R., 'Property speculators and the building of Glasgow 1780–1830', *Scottish Journal of Political Economy*, 8 (1961), 211–32. The land market and Scottish tenure attributed considerable explanatory importance to the development of Glasgow based on a penetrating case study of the Hutcheson estates.

Kellett, J. R., *The Impact of Railways on Victorian Cities* (1969). Generalisations based on five meticulous case studies of much wider significance to urbanisation than title suggests.

Kenwood, A. G., 'Residential building activity in north-eastern England 1853–1913', *Manchester School*, 31 (1963), 115–28. Convincingly argues that changes in local rather than national economic conditions influence housebuilding activity.

Lambert, R., *Sir John Simon 1816–1904 and English Social Administration* (1963). With Wohl (1983) provides excellent account of health and sanitary background to housing.

Law, C. M., 'The growth of urban population in England and Wales 1801–1911', *Transactions Institute of British Geographers*, 41 (1967), 125–43. Most widely quoted estimates of urban population percentages.

Laxton, P., 'Liverpool in 1801: a manuscript return for the first national census of population', *Transactions Historic Society of Lancashire and Cheshire*, 130 (1981), 73–113. Illuminating analysis of early social segregation and housing occupancy, despite the title.

Lewis, J. P., *Building Cycles and Britain's Growth* (1965). Most comprehensive summation of building fluctuations. Detailed appendices contain rich local pickings.

McCord, N., 'Ratepayers and Social Policy' in P. Thane (ed),

The Origins of British Social Policy (1978). Less substance than the title implies.

McKenna, J. and Rodger, R. G., 'Control by coercion: employers' associations and the establishment of industrial order in the building industry of England and Wales 1860–1914', *Business History Review*, 59 (1985), 213–31. Explains employers' collusive reactions to increasing labour costs. See Price (1980).

Maiwald, K., 'An index of building costs in the United Kingdom 1845–1938', *Economic History Review*, 7 (1954), 187–203. Still the most widely employed index despite dubious weighting of labour and materials on a constant 50–50 basis.

Marshall, J. D., 'Colonisation as a factor in the planting of towns in North-West England' in H. J. Dyos (ed.), *The Study of Urban History* (1968), pp. 215–30. Shows company housing developments retained their characteristics when absorbed by urban growth.

Melling, J. (ed.), *Housing, Social Policy and the State* (1980). Part of evolving socialist critique of capitalist production in context of house production and rentier incomes.

Melling, J., 'Employers, industrial housing and the evolution of company welfare policies in Britain's heavy industry: west Scotland 1870–1920 ', *International Review of Social History*, 26 (1981), 255–301. Downgrades the significance of paternalist employers and considers housing as part of employer-employee conflict (see Tarn, Daunton 1980).

Melling, J., *Rent Strikes: Peoples' Struggle for Housing in West Scotland 1890–1916* (Edinburgh, 1983). Highlights the power and capability of women to mobilise a political campaign to oppose rent increases.

Morgan, N. J. and Daunton, M. J., 'Landlords in Glasgow: a study of 1901', *Business History*, 25 (1983), pp. 264–81. Examines implications of distinctive concentration of property management in Scotland.

Morris, R. J., 'The middle class and the property cycle during the industrial revolution' in T. C. Smout (ed.), *The Search for Wealth and Stability* (1979). Concludes that in middle age, professional groups preferred property to equity investment as the basis for dependable incomes in their old age.

Morris, R. J., 'The middle class and British towns and cities of the industrial revolution 1780–1870' in D. Fraser and A. Sutcliffe (eds) (1983), pp. 286–306. Analyses power base of middle class and demonstrates their interest in creating nineteenth-century towns.

Morris, R. J., 'Urbanization', in J. Langton and R. J. Morris (eds), *Atlas of Industrializing Britain 1780–1914* (1986). Maps and diagrams offer visual dimension to residential segregation, economic functions, growth of public utilities and urban transport in towns.

Mortimore, M. J., 'Landownership and urban growth in Bradford and environs in the West Riding conurbation 1850–1950', *Transactions Institute of British Geographers*, 46 (1969), 105–19. Contends builders on freehold land were more financially constrained compared to those with leasehold land and so built to a greater density.

Murray, B. K., 'The politics of the "People's Budget"', *Historical Journal*, 16 (1973), 555–70. With Gilbert integrates 'parasitic landlords' into the historiography of constitutional crisis.

Muthesius, S., *The English Terraced House* (New Haven, 1982). Lavishly illustrated architectural account of internal and external design changes to English housing.

Offer, A., *Property and Politics 1870–1914: Landownership, Law, Ideology and Urban Development in England* (Cambridge, 1981). Cogent argument for an Edwardian property crisis. Integrates housing into the mainstream of late-Victorian political currents. Should be read in conjunction with Englander, Daunton (1983), Murray and Gilbert.

Olsen, D. J., 'House upon house: estate development in London and Sheffield', in H. J. Dyos and M. Wolff (eds) (1973), vol. 1, pp. 333–57. Contrasts landowners' strategies.

Olsen, D. J., *The Growth of Victorian London* (1976). An important study of physical development and social segregation in London with the aesthetic moral basis of Victorian society also considered.

Perkin, H. J., 'The "social tone" of Victorian seaside resorts in the north west', *Northern History*, 11 (1975), 180–94. Relegates transport and emphasises landowners' influence on urban configuration.

Pointing, J. E. and Bulos, M. A., 'Some implications of failed issues of social reform: the case of leasehold enfranchisement', *International Journal of Urban and Regional Research*, 8 (1984), 467–80. Argues that a 'conservative consensus' emerged in the mid 1880s which rallied support for aristocratic land-ownership and fought off radical Liberal land reforming interests. See also Reeder (1961).

Pooley, C. G., 'Residential mobility in the Victorian city', *Transactions Institute of British Geographers*, 4 (1979), 258–77. Identifies principal components of intra-urban mobility but maintains short-distance moves aided community stability.

Pooley, C. G., 'Housing for the poorest poor: slum clearance and rehousing in Liverpool 1890–1918', *Journal of Historical Geography*, 11 (1985), 70–88. Argues that despite ideological intent to rehouse the very poor, financial constraints made this impossible and municipal tenants were also selected largely on their ability to pay rent regularly. See Steffel, Gaskell (1976).

Powell, C. G., *An Economic History of the British Building Industry 1815–1979* (1980). Straightforward descriptive introduction.

Powell, C. G., 'He that runs against time: life expectancy of building firms in nineteenth century Bristol', *Construction History*, 2 (1986), 61–7. Concludes that the life expectancy of firms in the first half of the nineteenth century remained much the same.

Price, R., *Masters, Unions and Men: Work Control in Building and the Rise of Labour 1830–1914* (Cambridge, 1980). Contends that pressures and changes in the workplace altered the institutional structures on which labour power was founded.

Pritchard, R. M., *Housing and the Spatial Structure of the City: Residential Mobility and the Housing Market in an English City since the Industrial Revolution* (Cambridge, 1976). Spatial models analysed in the case of Leicester.

Ravetz, A., 'The Victorian coal kitchen and its reforms', *Victorian Studies*, 11 (1968), 435–60. Integrates technical change, consumer market and kitchen design, and argues that coal ranges dominated kitchens until 1914.

Reeder, D. A., 'The politics of urban leaseholds in late Victorian England', *International Review of Social History*, 6 (1961), 413–30. Leasehold system examined in relation to Liberal reform·

ers' attempts to restructure the interests of landowners, landlords and labour. Read with Pointing and Bulos, Gilbert, Murray.

Reeder, D. A., 'A theatre of suburbs: some patterns of development in west London 1801–1911' in H. J. Dyos (ed.), *The Study of Urban History* (1968), pp. 253–71. Diversity of suburbanisation examined in relation to Hammersmith and Paddington. Emphasises how residential composition affected social and religious institutions, recreational and other features.

Rimmer, W. G., 'Alfred Place Terminating Building Society, 1825–1843', *Thoresby Society Publications*, 46 (1963), 303–30. Neglected account of the mechanics of early building societies.

Rimmer, W. G., 'Working mens' cottages in Leeds 1770–1840', *Thoresby Society Publications*, 46 (1963), 165–99. Read with Beresford. Explains deteriorating housing before 1840 as a result of inadequate investment in social overhead capital – streets, sewers, cleansing – not constructional standards.

Roberts, E., 'Working class housing in Barrow and Lancaster 1880–1930', *Transactions Historic Society of Lancashire and Cheshire*, 127 (1977), 109–31. Argues that public pressure (Barrow) and paternalism (both towns) rather than council building advanced housing standards.

Rodger, R. G., 'Speculative builders and the structure of the Scottish building industry 1860–1914', *Business History*, 21 (1979), 226–46. Stresses dependence on small-scale building firms north of the border.

Rodger, R. G., ' "The invisible hand" – market forces, housing and the urban form in Victorian cities' in D. Fraser & A. Sutcliffe (eds) (1983), 190–211. Explains why tenements rather than terraced housing developed in Scotland.

Rodger, R. G., 'The Victorian building industry and the housing of the Scottish working class' in M. Doughty (ed.), *Building the Industrial City* (Leicester, 1986), pp. 151–206. Relates physical features of buildings to the social behaviour and physiological charactericstics of residents.

Rose, D., 'Accumulation versus reproduction in the inner city: the recurrent crisis of London revisited' in M. Dear and A. J. Scott (eds), *Urbanization and Urban Planning in Capitalist Society*

(1981), pp. 339–81. Reproduction of labour and capital accumulation explain housing crisis and capitalist mode of production prevents a solution. See also essays by Mollenkopf, Walker, Harvey and Cox.

Rubinstein, D., *Victorian Homes* (Newton Abbot, 1974). Judiciously chosen contemporary extracts provide useful insights into most aspects of Victorian housing.

Saul, S. B., 'Housebuilding in England 1890–1914', *Economic History Review*, 15 (1962), 119–37. Variations in credit and vacant houses stressed in preference to international capital flows as determinants of building fluctuations.

Simpson, M. A. and Lloyd, T. H. (eds), *Middle Class Housing in Britain* (Newton Abbot, 1977). Essays by Newton (Exeter), Simpson (Glasgow), Thompson (Hampstead), Lloyd (Leamington), Edwards (Nottingham) and Tarn (Sheffield). Variable quality of contributions and the lack of an editorial synthesis fails to achieve for middle-class what Chapman (1971) did for working-class housing.

Smith, P. J., 'Planning as environmental improvement: slum clearance in Victorian Edinburgh' in A. Sutcliffe (ed.), *The Rise of Modern Urban Planning 1800–1914* (1980), pp. 99–133. Interprets small-scale clearance schemes as progressive precursors of planning.

Springett, J., 'Land development and house-building in Huddersfield, 1770–1911', in M. Doughty (ed.), *Building the Industrial City* (Leicester, 1986). Explains the decline of the dominant Ramsden landowners in terms of building industry responses to redefined market opportunities.

Steffel, R. V., 'The Boundary Street Estate: an example of urban redevelopment by the London County Council 1889–1914', *Town Planning Review*, 47 (1976), 161–73. Detailed critique of LCC's policies. See also Allan, Smith.

Summers, A., 'A home from home – women's philanthropic work in the nineteenth century' in S. Burman (ed.), *Fit Work for Women* (1979). A useful survey of house-to-house visiting and the offerings of bibles, menus and advice intended to provide material and spiritual comfort.

Summerson, J., *Georgian London* (1945). Pathbreaking study continued into Victorian period by Olsen (1976), though not confined to housing.

Sutcliffe, A., 'Working class housing in nineteenth century Britain: a review of recent research', *Bulletin Society for the Study of Labour History*, 24–5 (1972), 40–51. Useful bibliographical survey to 1972.

Sutcliffe, A. (ed.), *Multi-Storey Living: the British Working Class Experience* (1974). Examines English flat-dwelling tradition in varied locations; stronger Scottish tradition receives scant attention.

Sutcliffe, A., *Towards the Planned City: Germany, Britain, the United States and France 1780–1914* (1981). Less rosy, but like Ashworth, Cherry and Tarn, basically optimistic view of planning.

Swenarton, M., *Homes Fit For Heroes: The Politics and Architecture of Early State Housing in Britain* (1981). First two chapters deal with innovations in housing design, garden cities and public housing before 1914.

Swenarton, M. and Taylor, S., 'The scale and nature of the growth of owner-occupation in Britain between the wars', *Economic History Review*, 38 (1985), 373–92. Recalculates Cleary's guess of 10 per cent and upwardly revises to 14–23 per cent for owner occupation in 1914.

Tarn, J. N., *Working Class Housing in 19th-century Britain* (1971). Despite title mainly concerned with charitable housing initiatives. Familiarised historians with design features and their impact on domestic life through extensive use of scale drawings.

Tarn, J. N., *Five Per Cent Philanthropy: An Account of Housing in Urban Areas between 1840 and 1914* (Cambridge, 1973). Plates and scale drawings add to the most comprehensive account of model dwellings movement (see also Gaskell 1987).

Taylor, I. C., 'The court and cellar dwelling: the eighteenth century origin of the Liverpool slum', *Transactions Historic Society of Lancashire and Cheshire*, 122 (1970), 67–90. Clear explanation of housing types with important nineteenth-century overlap.

Taylor, I. C., 'The insanitary housing question and tenement dwellings in nineteenth century Liverpool', in A. Sutcliffe (ed.) (1974), pp. 41–87. Clear account of the origins of housing problems.

Thomas, B., *Migration and Economic Growth* (1954). Influential study of building cycles which argues for systematic inter-national transfer and equalisation of capital and labour (see also Cairncross). Saul and Habakkuk offer the most powerful critique; Lewis the widest examination of Thomas's thesis.

Thompson, F. M. L., *Hampstead. Building a Borough 1650–1914* (1974). Typically elegant prose traces estate development in Hampstead and architectural entity despite fragmented ownership pattern.

Thompson, F. M. L. (ed.), *The Rise of Suburbia* (Leicester, 1982). Expansive introduction not matched by myopic contributors – Carr (Bexley), Rawcliffe (Bromley), Jahn (Ealing, Acton), and a lone provincial study by Treen (North Leeds).

Treble, J. H., *Urban Poverty in Britain 1830–1914* (1979). General-ises beyond G. S. Jones's analysis of London labour market and emphasises widespread frequency of interrupted wages as a central cause of poverty.

Trowell, R., 'Speculative housing development in the suburbs of Headingley, Leeds 1838–1914', *Thoresby Society Publications*, 59 (1985), 50–118. Claims that architects played a significant part in suburban design and layout, so builders were not reliant on pattern books for their designs.

Waller, P. J., *Town, City and Nation: England 1850–1914* (Oxford, 1983). Most comprehensive synthesis on urbanisation after 1850.

Ward, D., 'Victorian cities: how modern?', *Journal of Historical Geography*, 1 (1975), 135–51. Argues that residential segrega-tion was less developed than historians claim.

Ward, D., 'The Victorian slum: an enduring myth', *Annals Association American Geographers*, 66 (1976), 323–36. Questions the validity of the term 'slum', and argues it was a construct of the changing social geography of the Victorian city in which the poor were defined by reformers as a deviant group.

Ward, D., 'Environs and neighbours in the "Two Nations": residential differentiation in mid-nineteenth century Leeds', *Journal of Historical Geography*, 6 (1980), 133–62. Contrary to Dennis, Laxton, Pooley, discovers less social segregation in Leeds in 1870 compared to 1840.

Ward, J. R., 'Speculative building at Bristol and Clifton 1783–1793', *Business History*, 20 (1978), 3–18. Clear exposition of the building process, bankruptcies and inter-relatedness with local economy.

Weber, B., 'A new index of residential construction and long cycles in housebuilding in Great Britain 1838–1950', *Scottish Journal of Political Economy*, 2 (1955), 104–32. The most authoritative index of building based on an innovative indexing technique (subsequently incorporated and expanded by Lewis).

Weber, B. 'A new index of house rents for Great Britain 1874–1913', *Scottish Journal of Political Economy*, 7 (1960), 232–7 and three comparative series, *SJPE*, 8 (1961), 64. Refines earlier indices.

White, J., *Rothschild Buildings: Life in an East End Tenement Block 1887–1920* (1980). Illuminating oral history of life in purpose-built Jewish immigrant housing.

Whitehand, J. W. R., 'Building activity and the intensity of development at the urban fringe: the case of a London suburb in the nineteenth century', *Journal of Historical Geography*, 1 (1975), 211–24. Uniquely argues that for land-extensive users (institutions) and land-intensive ones (housing) proportionate site costs vary and are related to the building cycle. For debate see Daunton, Whitehand, Rodger, *JHG*, 4 (1978), 175–91, and 5 (1979), 72–8.

Whitehand, J. W. R., *The Changing Face of Cities: A Study of Development Cycles and Urban Form* (Oxford, 1987). See above and Conzen (1981). A synthesis of some 17 previous papers on land prices and their relationship to building development.

Wohl, A. S., *The Eternal Slum: Housing and Social Policy in Victorian London* (1977). Penetrating analysis of much wider significance than London alone.

Wohl, A. S., *Endangered Lives: Public Health in Victorian Britain* (1983). Investigates noise, industrial disease, smoke and other pollutants to conclude that though the urban population succumbed less to epidemic disease in 1914 than at the start of the Victorian age, it remained far from healthy.

Yelling, J. A., *Slums and Slum Clearance in Victorian London* (1986). Assesses impact of Cross's Act in London, and claims that it produced a crucial review of housing policy and municipal intervention. Heavy reliance on Boundary Street scheme.

Index